Fragmentation in International Human Rights Law

This book explores the effects of institutional fragmentation in international human rights law, by comparing the rights jurisprudence of three human rights courts and bodies, namely the European Court for Human Rights, the Inter-American Court for Human Rights and the Human Rights Committee. Contributions cover the areas of freedom of expression (journalism and the media), right to privacy, freedom of assembly and freedom of association (political parties), and measure the extent of fragmentation of human rights protection. Moreover, the volume argues that, while the conflict of laws approach, favoured by the International Law Commission, might work in avoiding conflicting obligations by states, in practice it is not an approach that presents a viable research agenda when it comes to understanding the causes and consequences of institutional fragmentation. This is especially evident in areas like international human rights, where there is a real possibility of a silent drift in the understanding of the nature of rights and the jurisprudence of an ever increasing number of international courts and bodies with human rights jurisdiction.

This book was originally published as a special issue of the *Nordic Journal of Human Rights*.

Marjan Ajevski is a Post-Doctoral Researcher at the PluriCourts Centre for the Research of the Legitimate Roles of the International Judiciary in the Global Order, Faculty of Law, University of Oslo, Norway.

Fragmentation in International Human Rights Law

Beyond conflict of laws

Edited by
Marjan Ajevski

Routledge
Taylor & Francis Group
LONDON AND NEW YORK

First published 2015 by Routledge

2 Park Square, Milton Park, Abingdon, Oxon OX14 4RN
711 Third Avenue, New York, NY 10017, USA

Routledge is an imprint of the Taylor & Francis Group, an informa business

First issued in paperback 2017

British Library Cataloguing in Publication Data
A catalogue record for this book is available from the British Library

ISBN 13: 978-1-138-90657-0 (hbk)
ISBN 13: 978-1-138-08473-5 (pbk)

Typeset in Adobe Garamond
by RefineCatch Limited, Bungay, Suffolk

Publisher's Note
The publisher accepts responsibility for any inconsistencies that may have arisen during the conversion of this book from journal articles to book chapters, namely the possible inclusion of journal terminology.

Contents

Citation Information

The chapters in this book were originally published in the *Nordic Journal of Human Rights*, volume 32, issue 2 (May 2014). When citing this material, please use the original page numbering for each article, as follows:

Chapter 1
Fragmentation in International Human Rights Law – Beyond Conflict of Laws
Marjan Ajevski
Nordic Journal of Human Rights, volume 32, issue 2 (May 2014) pp. 87–98

Chapter 2
Comparative International Human Rights Law: An Analysis of the Right to Private and Family Life across Human Rights "Jurisdictions"
Lucas Lixinski
Nordic Journal of Human Rights, volume 32, issue 2 (May 2014) pp. 99–117

Chapter 3
Freedom of Speech as Related to Journalists in the ECtHR, IACtHR and the Human Rights Committee – a Study of Fragmentation
Marjan Ajevski
Nordic Journal of Human Rights, volume 32, issue 2 (May 2014) pp. 118–139

Chapter 4
Comparative Freedom of Assembly and the Fragmentation of International Human Rights Law
Orsolya Salát
Nordic Journal of Human Rights, volume 32, issue 2 (May 2014) pp. 140–156

Chapter 5
Fragmentation in International Human Rights Law: Political Parties and Freedom of Association in the Practice of the UN Human Rights Committee, European Court of Human Rights and Inter-American Court of Human Rights
Svetlana Tyulkina
Nordic Journal of Human Rights, volume 32, issue 2 (May 2014) pp. 157–175

Please direct any queries you may have about the citations to
clsuk.permissions@cengage.com

Notes on Contributors

Marjan Ajevski is a Post-Doctoral Researcher at the PluriCourts Centre for the Research of the Legitimate Roles of the International Judiciary in the Global Order, Faculty of Law, University of Oslo, Norway.

Lucas Lixinski is a Senior Lecturer in the Faculty of Law at the University of New South Wales, Sydney, Australia.

Orsolya Salát is an Assistant Professor in the Faculty for Social Sciences, ELTE University Budapest, Budapest, Hungary, and Junior Research Fellow in the Institute for Legal Studies, HAS Centre for Social Sciences, Budapest, Hungary.

Svetlana Tyulkina is a Postdoctoral Research Fellow at the Gilbert & Tobin Centre of Public Law, Faculty of Law, University of New South Wales, Sydney, Australia.

Foreword

Andreas Follesdal

All princes and rulers of independent governments all through the world, are in a state of nature
(John Locke 1690: *Two Treaties on Government*, section 14)

The subject of this fascinating volume is the fragmentation of international and regional human rights courts and treaty bodies (ICs), that is, tensions *among* courts which all address the same functional area, often bringing apparently similar norms to bear. The rights of concern here are widely regarded as belonging to the core of human rights: freedom of expression (Ajevski II, 32–53), right to privacy (Lixinski, 13–31), freedom of assembly (Salát, 54–70) and freedom of association (Tyulkina, 71–89).

What are we to make of the conflicts that occur not only among such rights and other norms of international law – ranging from trade to the environment – but conflicts among the various human rights courts empower to adjudicate such rights – which courts and rights often conflict? The recent proliferation of international courts suggest that such intra-issue fragmentation will become more frequent, and solutions to the tensions more urgent. What exactly are the problems of fragmentation worth our concern? How are we to diagnose them, and what might count as fruitful paths toward their resolution?

I. What is the problem with conflicts among human rights ICs?

Is there reason to be concerned if several institutions which adjudicate the same norms come to different conclusions – as long as they seldom apply to the same cases? Indeed, some apparent fragmentation of this kind may be positive, for instance insofar as it reflects the diversity of values and alternatives within differing local circumstances (Lixinski, 25–26).

However, there are some such conflicts that may give rise to worry, insofar as they challenge the legitimacy of human rights ICs. At least three kinds of problems may arise.

Legitimacy of the international human rights judiciary. One important usage of the term 'legitimacy' concerns the reasons various agents have to defer to the decisions of particular authorities, in the face of other countervailing reasons. In our case: why should states heed judgements by international or regional human rights ICs? This is not only an abstract academic issue: several contributions in this volume mention states who refuse to engage with human rights ICs, or who consider withdrawing from the Inter-American Court of Human Rights (IACHR). So this is not a purely theoretical exercise. Insofar as the human rights ICs actually do engender conflicting judgements on the same or similar cases, the issue of legitimacy of course becomes crucial: what reasons do agents have to defer to one IC which claims authority rather than to another? Tyulkina describes one such case, where the freedom of association protected by Article 22 of the ICCPR, and by the ECtHR. This freedom is limited by Article 4(b) of the Convention on Elimination of Racial Discrimination, which requires

> States Parties to condemn all propaganda and all organizations which are based on ideas or theories of superiority of one race or group of persons of one colour or ethnic origin, or which attempt to justify or promote racial hatred and discrimination in any form, and undertake to adopt immediate and positive measures designed to eradicate all incitement to, or acts of, such discrimination and,. . . (b) shall declare illegal and prohibit [such] organizations

Conflicts among the treaty bodies as to how states should regulate freedom of expression and association are thus to be expected. This may require us to look at the reasons each of these authorities can claim that other actors defer, in various ways. Several approaches in legal theory address the reasons to defer to one institution rather than to another. Some approaches to resolve the tensions are canvassed in later sections of this introduction.

Stabilize expectations. In addition to the resolution of particular disputes, an important function of many ICs is to reduce their incidence in the future. They do so by increasing predictability about what international law requires, hence stabilizing parties' expectations about the behaviour of others. Such predictability is impossible insofar as there are conflicting judgments from different ICs about what the law requires. Thus the International Law Commission on fragmentation of international law notes,

> Fragmentation puts to question the coherence of international law. Coherence is valued positively owing to the connection it has with predictability and legal security. Moreover, only a coherent legal system treats legal subjects equally. (Koskenniemi 2006)

Confirm the universality of human rights. Many authors hold that human rights are universal, in that their normative grounds entail that they should be protected uniformly globally, across jurisdictions (Lixinski explores this on pp. 13–14). On this line of reasoning, the various human rights ICs should uphold similar norms, and arguably adhere to similar practices regarding the interpretation of and 'balancing' among rights. Discrepancies among ICs with different jurisdictions may thus challenge the normative standing of international human rights, even though these differences do not create proper legal conflicts.

How are we to understand, assess and alleviate such cases of fragmentation? To a philosopher, these concerns are reminiscent of Locke's argument for why individuals in the state of nature should agree to establish a state.

II. Human Rights institutions in a Lockean state of nature

It may be helpful to place these concerns within the larger more familiar frame of the fragmentation of international courts and tribunals adjudicating different functional areas (Young 2012). Both forms of fragmentation leave us, our states and our international courts in a Lockean state of nature. Actors – for John Locke, first and foremost individuals – face complex challenges of dispute resolution. Each enjoys legislative, executive and judicial authority, which create conflicts in the absence of authoritative dispute resolution bodies. To be sure, circumstances are less dire than in Thomas Hobbes' state of nature, where fear of unprovoked attack predominates, and the need for protection against such misdeeds is paramount. Lockean circumstances are less brutish and nasty: The presumption is that even absent institutions, "no one ought to harm another in his life, health, liberty, or possessions." (Locke 1963 (1690), sec 6). The prime problems are disagreements among actors of such good will, where "[t]here is no superiority or jurisdiction of one over another." Disagreements among them cannot be settled in such a state of nature, hence the rationale for dispute resolution institutions such as a state – and beyond. The relevance for international relations was clear to Locke:

> . . . all princes and rulers of independent governments all through the world, are in a state of nature
>
> (Locke 1963 (1690), section 14)

Several contributions to the study of international relations can be read as reassessing and addressing Locke's problem, often challenging the necessity of his solution – subjecting all parties to a shared supreme dispute resolution authority. Parallels and differences are legio to current discussions of the fragmentation of international law and international courts – including human rights courts. A brief, incomplete taxonomy may be in order

III. If it ain't broke . . .

How severe a problem is Locke's concern about the lack of dispute resolution mechanisms among autonomous actors? Conflicts among states aside, what about inter-issue conflicts among international courts in general, and conflicts among human rights courts in particular?

The literature on the problems of fragmentation of international law is overwhelming, further fuelled by the Study Group on Fragmentation of the International Law Commission, (Koskenniemi 2006). Some authors have argued that while such conflicts are interesting in theory, they seldom occur in practice. Ajevski's contribution in this volume addresses this claim. The possible problems may be of at least two kinds. Two or more international courts may have overlapping jurisdiction for the resolution of disputes. They may decide the same or similar cases differently, without an arbiter among them. While conflicts among the norms upheld by different international courts in general may be few, they do arise in the human rights area. Such cases might arise between the Human Rights Committee (HRC) and the European Court of Human Rights (ECtHR). The increase in human rights conventions and treaty bodies, combined with 'dynamic interpretation' of the former by the latter, have inter alia led to frequent needs to 'balance' international human rights against each other.

A second, more theoretical issue is more salient for human rights courts than many others. Insofar as the normative grounds for certain norms are claimed to be universal, they are challenged insofar as different international or regional courts adjudicate them differently. To illustrate: actors in Locke's state of nature are all normatively bound to do no harm. Presumably, such 'negative' human rights duties hold universally, and alleged breaches should not be adjudicated differently depending on jurisdiction – say, whether afflicted individuals and their state are subject to the ECtHR or the Inter-American Court of Human Rights. Different 'balancing' of rights to privacy versus rights to freedom of expression may lead 'compliance constituencies' to question the value of these rights, or the legitimate authority of either of the courts – or all three.

IV. How to assess solutions

Before moving to some of the paths proposed in response to the challenges of fragmentation, some criteria for acceptable solutions merits mention. First of all, more coherence and consistency is clearly a desiderata given the concern to secure finality and to stabilize expectations and predictability. However, coherence does not suffice for legitimacy or the sort of predictability of law worth securing. The International Law Commission on fragmentation of international law noted, correctly, that

> Coherence is, however, a formal and abstract virtue. For a legal system that is regarded in some respects as unjust or unworkable, no added value is brought by the fact of its being coherently so.
> (Koskenniemi 2006)

What substantive requirements should be put on a more coherent and normatively justifiable system of international courts and tribunals? I submit three interrelated standards which have been widely circulated in the history of international law:

Legitimacy. We need an account of why other institutions, authorities and individuals should defer to the judgements of these human rights ICs: what reasons are there to regard such judgments as reasons to act which displace the other reasons actors may have? In the spirit of Raz' 'service conception', we should expect these ICs to resolve disputes brought to them, in accordance with standards of legality. Their norms and interpretive practice should also be predictable and thus foster parties' future expectations.

Responsiveness. The institutions and authorities must be sufficiently responsive to the best interests of citizens, and they must be trusted to remain so over time. In Locke's parlance, and typical of contract theories of justice since, this is expressed as a requirement that the institutions as a whole must be justifiable to each, e.g. by respecting and promoting their interests at least as well as any alternative institutional arrangement likewise acceptable to each.

Human rights. One implication of such responsiveness is human rights protection. In the history of political thought, human rights norms – moral or legal – are defended as constraints on legitimate state authority, against standard threats that arise within a state system. Many argue that a less fragmented international legal order must at least not jeopardise such human rights protections domestically, and may possibly also uphold similar constraints on international organizations which now pose similar threats to the best interests of those subject to their authority. Some hold that human rights norms should enjoy primacy in cases of norm conflict (Grossman 2013) – which is not to say that this is currently the case (de Wet and Vidmar 2012).

V. Three approaches

Among the many proposed responses to such fragmentation of international law as there is, it is possible to discern at least three strands of relevance to the particular challenges of international human rights courts. Each of them have strengths and weaknesses.

A. Formal Hierarchy

Locke's solution to the anarchy of the state of nature is famously to establish a formal hierarchy. All formerly independent agents will find it in their interest to transfer parts of their authority to a common authority – on certain conditions to protect against human rights abuses, as we would say today (Locke 1963 (1690), sec 89). Against this response at least three challenges are obvious. Firstly, we may now point to other alternatives which may provide sufficiently authoritative dispute resolution, rendering the hierarchy less obvious as the sole solution.

A second concern is the risks of creating a new source of domination and imperialism. How can we prevent abuse of such a supreme authority, especially if conjoined with centralized enforcement powers?

The third worry is that even if such a supreme authoritative international court could work in theory, it cannot work in practice. The International Law Commission Study group thus insisted that

> *no homogenous, hierarchical meta-system is realistically available to do away with such problems.* International law will need to operate within an area where the demands of coherence and reasonable pluralism will point in different directions. (Koskenniemi 2006, section 491)

B. Federalism

Another family of responses to fragmentation explores non-unitary political and legal arrangements, in the form of confederal or federal orders. In such arrangements authority is constitutionally dispersed between a centre and member units, often on a territorial basis. This can prevent conflicting jurisdictions, protect against domination by central authorities – and still secure sufficient joint action where required e.g. according to a Principle of Subsidiarity. Thus Kant favoured a confederation of liberal republics; optimists look to the EU as the embryo of such a complex order.

For our purposes, to reduce fragmentation human rights courts can be placed and circumscribed at three levels:

- International, e.g. UN norms and treaty bodies such as the Human Rights Committee.
- Regional – including the IACHR and the ECtHR.
- Domestic authorities which may judge human rights compliance, and enjoy some discretion in this regard in the form of a 'margin of appreciation' concerning whether norms are violated.

Among the crucial challenges to these strategies is firstly how to divide competences among the various units. Considerations of subsidiarity may structure some such debates about how to distribute and redistribute authority, but this is still difficult for issue areas which overlap – such as when trade agreements appear to conflict with human rights. Secondly, who is to perform such assessments and readjustments concerning the comparative benefits of central and local action – including decisions about which are the objectives to be promoted?

C. Informal Network – 'judicial dialogue'

A third category of responses to reduce fragmentation is various forms of more informal means whereby actors come to agreement, take steps to avoid conflicts, or agree to be guided by principles of interpretation that seek to promote consistency. Anne Marie Slaughter's work on networks of judges is one of several interesting contributions in this broad category (Slaughter 2004). As a result, when arguing and judging about a case, the judges may come to regard themselves as members of a global – or regional – judiciary, rather than delegates or trustees of the national legal systems.

Another range of means to reduce fragmentation which international – and national – courts resort are several less formal principles and techniques in response to such negative effects of fragmentation as there may be (Nollkaemper and Fauchald 2012). One partial solution is shared standards and practices of interpretation (cf Koskenniemi 2006, Alvarez 2013). Some such self-imposed principles of interpretation are those maintained by the IACHR as quoted by Lixinski (pp. 18–19):

> the provision of its instruments, including the American declaration, should be interpreted and applied within the context of the inter-American and international human rights systems and, in the broader sense, in the light of the evolution of international human rights law.

The contributions in this volume bring out several ways that such networks may address intra-sector fragmentation among the human rights courts. However, this general strand of responses raises important questions both as to the legality and the results of such networks (cf Anderson 2005). How can networks avoid the risk that they reach agreement not on the basis of the best reasons but in recognition of power differentials and under the shadow of mutual assured destruction – where the judges of the various courts know that their legitimacy depends on avoiding such blatant conflicts. Why, in short, should citizens regard themselves as morally bound to obey the results? In response, I submit that some of these modes of informal harmonization can reduce rather than increase such risks.

Migration of norm interpretation. Several or all courts may come to borrow definitions or interpretations. Thus the definition of 'terrorism' has been picked up by various ICs (Husabø 2008). Similarly, human rights might be dynamically interpreted to include environmental preconditions for life, physical integrity. However, Lixinski finds little evidence of such migration (Lixinski, p. 23 and p. 26). Limitations of human rights may similarly be borrowed across jurisdictions: The IACHR apparently added as a condition on permissible exemptions that they must be necessary 'in a democratic society' – a condition borrowed from the European Convention on Human Rights (*inter alia* art. 8, 9, 10, 11) – as discussed by Lixinski (p. 19) and Ajevski (II, pp. 41–42).

Migration of 'balancing' of human rights norms. Among the particularly difficult areas of fragmentation among human rights courts are practices of 'balancing' among human rights norms. The term 'balancing' is unfortunate (Cali 2007), not least because it conveys an impression of a mechanical and value neutral process. What counts as acceptable restriction on one right for the sake of other rights is a more complex issue, where judges must resort to discretion. Thus Raz holds that

> Often, instead of following one rule rather than the other, practical conflicts should be resolved by finding the option that satisfies the conflicting rules to the highest possible degree. That follows from the nature of practical rationality, which requires that when reasons cannot be completely conformed to, they should be conformed to, to the highest possible degree. This will require courts confronted with conflicts of this kind to find such an optimific outcome, which will involve an understanding of the point of the conflicting rules. . . .
>
> Even so, not infrequently in different rules of law conflicts, the law does not contain the resources to resolve the conflict. It is indeterminate regarding the issue, usually leaving such decisions to the discretion of judges, i.e., to their judgment about the real merit of the different rules, a judgment that goes beyond what the law determines.
>
> (Raz 2006, 1023–25)

This underscores the worry mentioned above: how can we reduce the risk of domination – to be subject to judges' arbitrary discretion in such hard cases? And how reduce the attendant risk of variations in judgments as regards such 'universal' rights?

The first response is of course, that many hold that such discretion should be limited to when other legal rules are exhausted, so that the incidents are infrequent. In addition, several procedural requirements can constrain the discretion of judges – procedures which themselves also can migrate. Thus authors in this volume hold that the *existence of* and *components* of a proportionality test to assess whether a rights violation is permitted, themselves are imported across jurisdictions (cf Lixinski on the case of Cuba, p. 20). Another example is the ECtHR' practice of reducing the margin of appreciation it grants states, when it detects an 'emerging European consensus' on the issue – be it the prohibition of physical punishment in schools (1978, Rasmussen v Denmark 8777/79 (ECtHR 28. nov. 1984), para 40); X v United Kingdom 75/1995/581/667 Eur Ct HR (European Court of Human Rights), 13). Such respect for the member states' expressed values help reduce the risk of domination of judges – insofar as such consensus is not only in the eyes of the beholder (Helfer 1993, 154).

VI. Concluding Remarks

The contributions of this volume provide a refreshing stimulus to diagnose some of the fascinating challenges to the system of states by the developments of international law – how to secure unity among multiple international human rights courts, whilst also ensuring appropriate diversity reflecting legitimate variations among states. The precursors of these chapters were first discussed at an authors' workshop convened by Marjan Ajevski at the Central European University in Budapest May 16, 2013. The workshop and this volume is part of the European Research Council Advanced Grant activities MultiRights, concerning the legitimacy of the multi-level human rights regimes. The analyses, suggestions and prescriptions offered by these authors may help render our emerging multi-level legal and political order more comprehensible and legitimate – and thereby somewhat more worthy of our deference.

References

(1978). *Tyrer vs. United Kingdom*, ECtHR. **Series A No. 26.**

Anderson, K. (2005). "Squaring the circle? Reconciling sovereignty and global governance through global government networks – review of Slaughter 2004." *Harvard Law Review*. 1255–1312. http://www.wcl.american.edu/faculty/anderson/docs/squaring.pdf?rd=1

Ajevski, M. (2014 I). "Fragmentation in International Human Rights Law – Beyond Conflict of Laws." 32 *Nordic Journal of Human Rights* 87.

Ajevski, M. (2014 II). "Freedom of Speech as Related to Journalists in the ECtHR, IACtHR and the Human Rights Committee – a Study of Fragmentation." 32 *Nordic Journal of Human Rights* 118.

Cali, B. (2007). "Balancing human rights: Methodological problems with weights, scales and proportions." *Human Rights Quarterly*. 251–270.

de Wet, E. and J. Vidmar, Eds. (2012). *Hierarchy in international law: The place of human rights*. Oxford, Oxford University Press.

Fauchald, O.K. and Nollkaemper, A., Eds. (2012). *The Practice of International and National Courts and the (De-)Fragmentation of International Law*. Oxford, Hart Publishing.

Grossman, N. (2013). "The normative legitimacy of international courts." *Temple Law Review* 86. http://papers.ssrn.com/sol3/papers.cfm?abstract_id=2185304 http://sites.temple.edu/lawreview/article/the-normative-legitimacy-of-international-courts/.

Helfer, L. (1993). "Consensus, Coherence and the European Convention on Human Rights." *Cornell international law journal* 133.

Husabø, E. J. (2008). The interaction between global, regional and national regulation in the definition of terrorism. *Multilevel Regulation and the EU: The interplay between Global, Europan and National normative processes.* A. Follesdal, R. Wessel and J. Wouters. Leiden, Martinus Nijhoff: 169–184.
Koskenniemi, M. (2006). Fragmentation of International Law: difficulties arising from the diversification and expansion of international law. *International Law Commission, Study Group on Fragmentation.*
Lixinski, L. (2014). "Comparative International Human Rights Law: An Analysis of the Right to Private and Family Life across Human Rights 'Jurisdictions'." 32 *Nordic Journal of Human Rights* 99.
Locke, J. (1963 (1690)). *Two treatises of government.* New York, New American Library, Mentor.
Raz, J. (2006). "The Problem of Authority: Revisiting the Service Conception." *Minnesota Law Review* 90: 1003–1044.
Salát, O. (2014). "Comparative Freedom of Assembly and the Fragmentation of International Human Rights Law." 32 *Nordic Journal of Human Rights* 140.
Tyulkina, S. (2014). "Fragmentation in International Human Rights Law: Political Parties and Freedom of Association in the Practice of the UN Human Rights Committee, European Court of Human Rights and Inter-American Court of Human Rights." 32 *Nordic Journal of Human Rights* 157.
Young, M. A., Ed. (2012). *Regime interaction in international law: Facing fragmentation.* Cambridge, Cambridge University Press.

Fragmentation in International Human Rights Law – Beyond Conflict of Laws

Marjan Ajevski

I. The Hydra that is Fragmentation

Like tackling the mythical hydra, the attempt of defining fragmentation is fraught with peril. It seems that once one solves one head of complexity, two more pop up in its place. The struggle for definition starts with the idea of the existence of a unified legal order, that of international law, which is under threat of shattering under the pressure of divergent "self-contained" regimes. These regimes, the story goes, have their own law-making and law application rules and mechanisms as well as "rules concerning the consequences of breaches of their respective primary norms".[1] However, once we start looking at how "self-contained" these regimes really are, we immediately notice their inter-relatedness in assumptions, sources, methods etc. both with general international law and amongst themselves.[2] So much for "autonomous systems decoupled from general international law".[3] But this does not cure international lawyers' anxieties,[4] unfortunately, for while these regimes may not be completely separate from international law, they still somehow threaten its unity by their ability to pronounce on issues relevant to international law and to do so in a way that conflicts with each other. In the proverbial state of nature without a hierarchical centre, what is to stop a normative conflict from ensuing, or so the fear goes.

Even if "self-contained" regimes do not, as such, exist, regimes certainly do. Of course, pinning down what exactly we mean by a regime – even a special one – as it turns out is not an easy feat. The International Law Commission found at least three ways in which the term is used:

> Sometimes violation of a particular group of (primary) rules is accompanied by a special set of (secondary) rules concerning breach and reactions to breach. This is the main case provided for under article 55 of the articles on Responsibility of States for internationally wrongful acts. Sometimes, however, a special regime is formed by a set of special rules, including rights and obligations, relating to a special subject matter. Such rules may concern a geographical area (e.g. a treaty on the protection of a particular river) or some substantive matter (e.g. a treaty on the regulation of the uses of a particular weapon). Such a special regime may emerge on the basis of a single treaty, several treaties, or treaty and treaties plus non-treaty developments (subsequent practice or customary law).

> Finally, sometimes all the rules and principles that regulate a certain problem area are collected together so as to express a "special regime". Expressions such as "law of the sea", "humanitarian law", "human rights law", "environmental law" and "trade law", etc. give expression to some such regimes. For interpretative purposes, such regimes may often be considered in their entirety. [footnotes omitted][5]

But even this taxonomy does not seem all that clear since the narrowest (first) definition fails the test with international criminal law, for example, for it can fit both the first and the third definition as it has a special set of primary rules for which the violation of "is accompanied by a special set of (secondary) rules concerning breach and reactions to breach".[6] Just think of the obligation of all states to prevent and punish genocide as part of the primary rules on genocide found in the genocide convention, not to mention all the other specificities like individual criminal responsibility, lack of reciprocity in its implementation etc. The Convention stakes out the crime of genocide, its *mens rea* and *actus reus* and prescribes both individual and state responsibility for those acts. It is both a very large part of international criminal law as a branch of international law in the third sense but it is also a single convention that outlines rules and responsibilities for states *and* individuals. The invocation of Hart's primary and secondary rules analogy seems unhelpful for all of these layers of regimes have primary and secondary rules to some extent, the main difference being whether your particular point of view is from the inside or outside of the regime. From inside, the European Union regimes seems quite reified and autonomous, state-like almost, until one is presented with the *Kadi* Court of First Instance[7] and European Court of Justice[8] judgments and the outside/inside perspective that they offer.

The discussion on fragmentation seems to be further complicated by the introduction of another kind of fragmentation, institutional fragmentation. So far we have been talking about substantive fragmentation, the separation of "law into highly specialized 'boxes' that claim relative autonomy from each other and from general law"[9] – hence the idea of human rights law, humanitarian law, law of the sea, the regime governing the river Danube etc. But the proliferation of different institutions within these "specialised boxes" (especially the box in its widest sense) adds a further twist to the story and another layer of anxiety for order-inclined lawyers since the existence of different institutions pronouncing on the meaning of the norms of those same boxes may, inevitably, lead to further specialisation into smaller and smaller boxes trying to occupy the same space. In a sense, it increases the problem exponentially since every new institution has the potential of interacting with every other.

The problems of international human rights and international criminal law seem to be particularly acute in this sense since while they rest on an assumption of normative unity due to their allegiance to the Universal Declaration on Human Rights, this presumption can easily be threatened by increasing the number of institutions that can authoritatively pronounce on the meaning of the regime norms. It seems in international human rights and international criminal law this presumptive unity can not only be shattered from the "outside" – by another regime taken in its widest sense – but, and probably more dangerously, from the "inside" by one of the sibling institutions. The proliferation of the UN system of right protection adds a further layer to the institutional dimension of fragmentation since not only do these human rights bodies cover normatively quite similar norms and topics with other human rights institutions outside the UN system, but with human rights bodies within the UN system itself.

II. The Conflict Bias

Similar to survivor bias,[10] fragmentation talk has its conflict bias or interaction bias. Let me explain. Survivors' bias is a bias that skews results by the mere fact of looking at instances of success. For instance, during World War II, what was to become the US Air Force wanted to know where to place additional armour most effectively on its bomber aircraft in order to increase the survivability of both crew and aircraft. The samples that they had to use to identify the vulnerable areas on the planes were the bombers that had returned from their missions carrying the scars of their ordeal. Naturally, the military wanted to put the additional protection on those areas that showed the most damage. It was not until a very smart mathematician pointed out that the areas that were mostly affected by damage were the least ones to worry about since the planes suffered extensive damage to them but still managed to survive the flight back. It was the areas that were undamaged that needed re-enforcement since logic would dictate that the planes that did not make it back were most likely brought down by damage in those areas.[11] The same can be said with researching success in investment. If one focuses on the calculating and forecasting models of successful investors one runs the risk of finding genius where chance might be the better explanation if the failing investors were not also included in the study.

Similarly with the fragmentation debate, if the fear of fragmentation is that autonomous regimes, thanks to their internal mechanisms of law-making and law application, would become, well, autonomous then focusing on the visible points of interaction – on the conflict – would skew the perception towards over or under estimating the extent of the fragmentation or to the forces that might operate to mitigate fragmentation in the first place. Not only that, but once we frame the fragmentation debate into a debate about interaction or conflict, then our solution is the familiar conflict of laws rules.[12] The solution for a nail is a hammer.

This conflict or interaction bias has been pervasive in the literature and it is the default conclusion of the ILC Study Group.[13] The assumption is that the proliferation of regimes leads to some kind of divergence which breeds conflict, the conclusion being to focus on the visible points of interaction whether it is conflict of cross fertilisation. An attempt was made to overcome the focus of conflict and interaction with the study of Multi-Sourced Equivalent Norms (MSEN) performed by Tomer Broude and Yuval Shany.[14] In their study they defined MSEN as

> Two or more norms which are (1) binding upon the same international legal subjects; (2) similar or identical in their normative content; and (3) have been established through different international instruments of "legislative" procedures or are applicable in different substantive areas of the law.[15]

This certainly is a novel approach – it tries to play down the conflict and interaction part of fragmentation and does try to emphasise the identical normative content of the norms. However, it is still predicated on the same subject being covered by MSE norms with the background assumption of a latent conflict or interaction ensuing. It is geared toward answering a specific systemic question of points of contact between system entities grouped by the normative equivalence of the norms themselves. It is geared towards answering interaction problems not normative divergence or convergence research.

More recently, Philippa Webb takes a novel approach in her latest book[16] where she tries to track down three international law doctrines, genocide, immunities and use of force through their development in four jurisdictions: the International Court of Justice (ICJ), the

International Criminal Court (ICC), the International Criminal Tribunal for Yugoslavia (ICTY) and the International Criminal Tribunal for Rwanda (ICTR). She strives to answer the question of what lies ahead for international law: integration or fragmentation.

This study takes a similar approach with rights that are based on different conventions but are understood to be normatively equivalent – they are the same norms, it is the enforcement mechanism and actor that is different, so-called institutional fragmentation. The rationale is that the fear of fragmentation is no less mitigated when there are no visible points of conflict or interaction between the institutions since the lack of interaction might also mean that for some specific regimes there is no meeting point. For example, there is hardly a place where the European Court of Human Rights and the Inter-American Court of Human Rights can meet since both of them cover different regional groups of states, even though they share a normative source – normative equivalence if you will – through the Universal Declaration of Human Rights. Certainly, if that is the case then no amount of conflict of laws rules will mitigate this type of drift. Moreover, if there is close to no divergence between these systems then maybe a better solution to fragmentation may not be conflict of laws rules but rather pinpointing the conditions, structures, institutions that drive this convergence (provided that convergence is what we strive towards, a normative question that is not directly part of this study) and replicating them. In short, there is still a lot we do not know, but certainly focusing on interaction alone is not the only way forward. What happens when the only point of contact is the normative equivalence of the norms themselves as is the case with human rights?

III. The Focus of the Special Issue

The approach of the Special Issue is to look at the consequences of institutional fragmentation *within* a specific branch – that of international human rights law (IHR). There is a presumption of normative unity in IHR, to a large extent stemming from its shared commitment to the Universal Declaration on Human Rights.[17] Consequently, the understanding of the rights and the extent of their protection should be, in principle, if not identical then at least largely overlapping.

The study has employed functionalist comparative law methodology using small *n* studies of the most similar case[18] systems. The reason for this approach is that the study is an attempt to pinpoint whether the *practice* of the institutions – their interpretation and application of human rights norms – has led to fragmented human rights protection. The systems under study were the European Court of Human Rights, the Human Rights Committee and the Inter-American Court of Human Rights. The decision for examining these three jurisdictions was based on the fact that they are all courts taxed with interpreting and applying conventions that protect civil and political rights (most similar case study). There was some consideration of whether the African Court/Commission should be included in the study; it is after all, a regional system of rights protection just like the ECtHR and the IACtHR. Ultimately, however, two considerations tipped the scales for its exclusion: a conceptual and a practical one. As a practical consideration, the African Charter has three outright conceptual differences with the other conventions: (1) the Charter includes not only civil and political but social and economic rights; (2) the other conventions (except for ICCPR, article 1 which in itself has no direct connection with the other articles in it) are designed as rights of individuals while the Charter specifically protects individuals' and peoples' rights; and (3) the Charter includes duties resting upon individuals rather than the state, which the others do not. In that sense, the African system presents a problem from the viewpoint of the most similar cases approach since it is likely that the normative choices included during the drafting of the Charter would influence the African Court's/ Commission's practice. From a practical consideration, the inclusion of a fourth jurisdiction ran the risk of overburdening the study with information without a clear conceptual benefit.

Furthermore, the choice of jurisdictions was partly due to the study's specific approach that goes beyond the conflict of laws and regime interaction but at the same time remains mindful of it. The basic idea was to treat each of these systems as separate legal systems and compare how their jurisprudence has developed over time. It presupposed that these institutions serve similar functions – the interpretation and adjudication of human rights treaty norms that are normatively equivalent – and that in the performance of this function are faced with broadly similar issues and problems i.e. that they, at a minimum, protect civil and political rights but also issues relating to their specific situation of being an international body dealing with sovereign states with different level of institutional and democratic development.

The purpose of the comparison is to see the extent to which fragmentation is an issue in these jurisdictions not by focusing on instances of conflict or interaction, but rather on the black letter law developments (the principles and doctrines that each system has expounded during the interpretation and application of the respective conventions) in each system and comparing the similarities and differences between them. Consequently, the methodology used in the study is a comparative law methodology. It assumes that there already is fragmentation – the institutional kind where there is more than one institution without a hierarchical relationship, that can pronounce on the meaning of the normatively equivalent norms that are international human rights – and that the focus is on the question of assessing its extent.

With this approach, the focus of the case selection within the specific jurisdictions is not to find those cases that show how the specific regime interacts with its "outside" environment, but on the so called "leading cases" that develop the black letter law. What the focus on leading cases will hopefully reveal is the state of the law in the respective regime as a baseline for comparison of what is understood by, for instance, the right to have private correspondence in these three systems, in the hope that it will reveal the overlaps and/or divergence in the systems' understanding of the substantive rights. By focusing away from regime interaction it should be possible to see the unobserved forces that drive the potential convergence or divergence. While regime interaction is not the primary focus, it is not completely sidelined either. The choice of jurisdictions should allow for both since while there is almost no chance of interaction, of creating overlapping obligations on states in case of the European and the Inter-American Courts, there is a real chance that that might happen in relation to the HRC and the European and Inter-American Courts, respectively, as in the case of religious education in Norwegian schools in respect to the HRC and the ECtHR.[19]

Furthermore, this study tries to table the discussion of fragmentation versus pluralism (and even whether there is actually a choice between the two) and does not strive to answer whether more or less fragmentation/pluralism is normatively desirable, nor whether fragmentation/pluralism is better at staving off hegemonic tendencies or not.[20] What it does try to ascertain is the extent of fragmentation or the extent to which there is convergence or divergence in the understanding of the equivalent norms by these three bodies. This brings us to the issue of at what point can we reasonably say that there is convergence and/or divergence and, especially, at what point do we say that fragmentation in IHL is significant and that it matters?

The answer can be given in several layers. The first layer is that, despite the common dedication to the Universal Declaration, the three conventions that form part of this study have noticeably different wording when it comes to the specific rights in question, both in length and in structure. However, despite this difference, there are also striking similarities between them: for instance, all of them have the familiar wording of "no one shall be subjected to torture or inhumane or degrading treatment or punishment".[21] Are these differences or similarities enough to be meaningful or significant when it comes to the severity of fragmentation/pluralism?

The second layer of complexity lies in the issue of the similarity or difference of doctrines, tests and justifications. When deciding a case, courts use tests, substantive doctrines and justifications in order to argue and justify why a case was decided one way rather than another. If the presumption of normative equivalence holds, then one would expect that the different courts would use the same or similar tests, doctrines and/or justifications to argue and settle similar cases. On the other hand, if the courts use different doctrines, tests or justifications to decide similar cases, then it is hard to see where the normative equivalence would be.

A third layer of complexity lays in the outcome of cases. It is conceivable that despite textual, doctrinal etc. divergences, there is a significant overlap in the outcomes of cases. The opposite also might be true, that despite a high overlap between doctrines, tests and/or justifications there would be a significant divergence in the outcome of cases, one system finding violations where the others would not. In all of these layers the question to be asked is at what point does a divergence or convergence become significant? Does the fact that courts use similar doctrines and justifications, but arrive at different outcomes, matter when it comes to fragmentation?

For the purposes of this study, we can conclude that a significant overlap/convergence has taken place when the courts use the same or similar doctrines, tests and justifications to decide cases and, *vice versa*, that if courts use different doctrines, tests and justifications to handle similar cases then a significant divergence is in place, which brings into question the normative unity of human rights norms. There are both theoretical and practical reasons on why this level of similarity/difference matters.

The theoretical standpoint has to do with the issue of interpretation and its constraints. As it has been argued, law – and anything else for that matter that is expressed in terms of language – is indeterminate.[22] Texts – including laws, treaties etc. – have multiple meanings and judges make a "choice"[23] of applying one over others when deciding cases. The key insight of the indeterminacy thesis, however, is that indeterminacy is settled by people's beliefs, convictions in certain substantive worldviews – notions of the good life[24] – shared by interpretative communities (practices)[25] through which texts, laws, treaty provisions etc. gain their meaning. Only when mediated through these substantive worldviews do texts make sense. Consequently, the various elements internal to the practice that populate its four corners is what acts as a constraint on interpretation. In practices such as law, these elements, like the understandings of what is a treaty, what is a reservation, margin of appreciation, etc., give outlays of what it is possible to argue (and argue successfully) at any given time – the so called "weak constraints of practice".[26] If certain elements are not part of the argumentation and justifications of a case, while others not internal to the practice are, then the case itself becomes suspect for no other reason than simply by not falling within the understanding of what it is to "do" law.

It is for this reason that the focus on measuring convergence and divergence should be on tests, doctrines and justifications. It is not the case that if the courts use similar tests, doctrines and justifications then they will decide similar cases with the same outcome in all instances, but it is certainly safe to assume that this will be the situation in most of the cases that they decide. Moreover, the overlap (and *vice versa*) of substantive justifications should give a clear indication of the shared or divergent notions of the "good life" between these courts, increasing the likelihood of convergence or divergence, respectively.

Moreover, there is a further reason to focus on this level of the judicial decision rather than rely completely on the outcomes of the decisions and that is related to the nature of judging. In the course of deciding a case, judges are expected to use their discretion in determining the relevance of facts and how and which facts fall under which qualification. This is something that has been alluded to in the article of Orsolya Salát in this issue, and that is that cases can be decided this way or that because of the way that judges qualify certain factual patterns, peaceful assembly, non-peaceful assembly, peaceful in part etc., and there is a limitless supply of situations that the world can throw at us that judges have to grapple with. Having said that, what matters is not that the judges have decided two similar cases differently, but the reasons why they have decided to do so, since even the most similar cases can have circumstances both in the initial occurrence of the case as well as at the time and place of application. To put it another way, it might matter greatly which international system is deciding the case and the type of environment the court is working in, and the best way to gauge this is to look at the tests, doctrines and justifications that the different courts use, and not focus only or even predominately on outcomes. Outcomes matter, but they matter in the sense that they are the products of structures and arguments that are different in their purposes/intentions.

There are also practical reasons for focusing on this level of comparison. For instance, concentrating on textual similarity or difference, due to interpretative dynamics, would miss completely the added value that institutions bring to the human rights regime and would defeat the purpose of this study which is to focus on the issue of institutional fragmentation. Consequently, excluding the interpretative outcomes of the institutions themselves would be highly nonsensical.

More importantly there is also the practical limitation of the sheer volume of cases needed to be researched if one was to focus on outcomes alone. For instance, the ECtHR has 35,854 judgments,[27] which complicates any data collection efforts in terms of quantitative comparison since the cases would have to be coded not by outcome and the treaty article involved but by factual pattern and issues discussed at a minimum in order to control for the similarity of cases. It is not that such research is impossible – some, like Lupu and Voeten,[28] have managed to code in certain fashion the majority of cases in the ECtHR, although probably not under the criteria listed above[29] – but that such an effort was beyond the resources of this studies presented here.

The articles in this Special Issue highlight the complexities of the fragmentation issue, in no small part due to the complexity of law and human rights. What the articles show is that there is a high level of contextuality in the different courts' approaches to settling their cases. Depending on the rights involved (even depending on specific subsections of the rights in question) – whether the right is more or less controversial, whether the cases involve clear over-reaction by governments, whether the issue at stake is one of so called "third generation rights" (like indigenous people's rights or substantive equality) – the courts might have a high level of overlap in their doctrines and approaches, while elsewhere they might completely diverge. Where there is overlap, it seems that there is a high level of cross-referencing and migration of doctrines between these courts.

This brings me to the individual articles in this issue. Lixinski's article highlights one particular semblance of the fragmentation debate, the problem of perspective. In a sense Lexinski rightly points out that in essence there is no difference between the phenomenon we see as pluralism and the phenomenon we see as fragmentation – it is a difference in the point of observation. Fragmentation is a problem seen from above, maybe from the armchairs of traditional courts, like the International Court of Justice, while from below, or from the academic side, the world and the international system is plural, with different regimes ultimately following different sources of authority – a system that shuns deliberate order and in the true Hobbesian sense is anarchical. Of course, there are proposals in between these two polar opposites of a plural system that is respondent to the ultimate need of preservation of public autonomy.[30]

As an example, Lixinski takes two instances of the right to private and family life, the personal correspondence of prisoners, and environmental cases. He finds in large part convergence when it comes to the personal correspondence of prisoners in the three jurisdictions both in doctrine and in level of protection (outcomes). On the other hand, when it comes to environmental cases, the story becomes more complicated. The ECtHR handles environmental cases under the scope of article 8, which has turned into a catch-all article for issues that do not squarely fit into any of the other rights. The IACtHR and the HRC, on the other hand, put these issues in the scope of their right to life articles or, for the IACtHR, in the article related to the general enjoyment of rights. The intriguing issue here is not that these courts have dealt with environmental rights cases using different articles of their founding conventions but that they have dealt with them at all, given the fact that the conventions in question are devoted to civil and political rights – why have these courts decided even to tackle cases and issues that were clearly not part of their original mandate? What is it that is driving the courts' acceptance of environmental issues as part of their scope and agenda? Is it the failure of other regimes? Is it the desire to put their foot in the door of the next big global issue – a hegemonic desire?[31] Is it the notion that human rights permeate every issue and, therefore, cannot be resolved without taking rights-friendly approaches?

Ajevski's contribution takes a much narrower approach to the issue of fragmentation and the freedom of expression. He compares the reasoning of the three courts in terms of the scope, tests and justifications found in their reasoning and finds a significant overlap, at least in the narrow field of journalists and media. Two things seem to stabilise the jurisprudence of the three courts, the proportionality test and, to a somewhat larger extent, the substantive understanding of the purpose of free speech in a democracy. While the proportionality test is the formula through which the rights issues are resolved, it is the substantive understanding of the importance of the freedom of expression for maintaining plural and democratic societies that seems to drive the jurisprudential overlap. What is striking, according to Ajevski, is the three courts' devotion to a substantive view of democracy where rights are seen not only as enabling democratic decision-making but as a constraint on it as well. They see rights as both enabling democracy by protecting a vigorous and plural public sphere of deliberation, but also constraining majoritarian impulses by ensuring that democratic societies are also plural and equal in a substantive sense by protecting dissenting voices and minorities. He points to the margin of appreciation as a potential stepping stone in this seeming convergence of jurisprudence, the reasons being the doctrine's unpredictability and its recent attachment to the national trends of the Council of Europe members. A question then emerges: why would any other jurisdiction wish to follow or align itself with a jurisprudence that follows the national trends of a handful of states? Has the ECtHR, by adopting a reading of the margin of appreciation as one that has to follow the national trends of its members, shunned the Universal Declaration on Human Rights? Or does it, unselfconsciously, consider that the future of human rights is necessarily European, and that European trends are the most progressive ones?

Orsolya Salát's article tackles fragmentation of the freedom of assembly, a jurisprudentially under-utilised right. Because of the closeness in the issues of freedom of expression and freedom of assembly, judges across all jurisdictions have settled most issues of assembly under expression doctrines. For instance, the IACtHR does not have a single case on the freedom of assembly, she finds, even though protests and their suppression have been present in the Americas in the past. Moreover, she finds some doctrinal differences between the two remaining jurisdictions and poses a rather more significant question of perception: at what point do outcomes matter? When talking about the divergent route taken by the HRC and ECtHR in terms of the requirement of a prior permit for an assembly and what is defined as assembly, she points out

> The diverging approach [of the HRC and the ECtHR] to the assembly claims [or the applicants] can be either considered (i) a difference arising out of institutional fragmentation; or (ii) a wholly innocent contingency of the complaints – in one case explicitly referring to freedom of assembly next to freedom of expression, and not in the other; or (iii) a wholly innocent contingency of divergent regulation: the Queensland town requiring permit for even one-person public addresses, while in the Hungarian case, quite to the contrary, a notice could only be required if something could be qualified as an "assembly".[32]

In short, even the minute circumstances of a case may matter for its final outcome, and concentrating on outcomes alone (violation or non-violation of a right) is not enough of a clue to gauge the extent of fragmentation. In her final remarks, she points out some of the problems that comparative studies of this kind can encounter, and urges the awareness of the problems that international lawyers can encounter in using comparative methods and encourages them to familiarise themselves with the drawbacks of these methods in order to avoid, or at least minimise, them.

Last, but by no means least, Svetlana Tyulkina's article on the freedom of association in relation to political parties offers us a perspective that involves not just case-law regulation but soft law (at least when it comes to the ECHR and the Council of Europe) as well. She focuses on the key issue of political parties when discussing freedom of association – their banning. What she finds in her study is that the three jurisdictions share the same standards and tests and put the restrictions on political parties under the proportionality test which is anchored by the substantive understanding that "it is in the very best interest of any true democracy to encourage their active involvement in dialogue between governments and citizens".[33] The substantive notion of democracy again anchoring the jurisprudence of the three courts via the formula of the proportionality test. This does not mean that there is uniformity in approach; the ECtHR and the Council of Europe have taken great strides in regulating the banning of political parties, in effect normalising the conduct while at the same time minimising it. On the other hand, the UN system seems to be interested more in banning extreme parties advocating racial or ethnic hatred or extremism while at the same time lagging behind in regulating the conduct.

Overall, this study seems to raise more questions than it answers. The results regarding the extent of fragmentation are mixed, partly stemming from the lack of clarity of what the fear is that fragmentation poses. If it is the fact that different courts can come to conflicting results, that is no less of a problem in national jurisdictions – let us not forget the fractured way in which the French high courts responded to the ECtHR article 6 jurisprudence as relating to the Advocate General and its counterpart in the *Cour de Cassation* and *Counsil d'Etat*, respectively,[34] where the *Cour de Cassation* practically ostracised the Advocate General while the *Counsil d'Etat* made only minor, cosmetic changes. We should also not forget the fact that technically the regulation that was under review in the *Lautsi*[35] judgment was unconstitutional but because of its jurisdictional issues was not heard by the Constitutional Court but by the Administrative Court which ruled on its legality.[36] Neither France nor Italy considers themselves as having problems of fragmentation. Probably the reason for this is that the unity of their national system is never in doubt, there is no "other", no competitor to the French or Italian system, respectively, which can claim to have a right to decide in all matters French or Italian. Which brings us back to the issue of perspective highlighted by Lixinski – whether fragmentation is a problem may depend on where you are coming from, and, equally important, what your fears are. By embracing pluralism/fragmentation in a substantive sense, have we also forgone the universalist ideal, the notion that every human being is endowed with rights because of his or her inherent human dignity, regardless of the circumstances in which those rights are exercised?

What is also clear from this study is that to have a shared substantive understanding of rights matters matters a great deal if there is to be a shared understanding of the purpose and intent of rights – what the rights are for and what are they there to protect. Having a common formula (like the proportionality test) through which to answer the questions that come up during rights reviews also helps greatly. There is a dark cloud on the horizon, though, highlighted by the emerging trend of the ECtHR tying the margin of appreciation to a European consensus which overshadows a new question in the fragmentation debate that is quite pertinent in rights issues – why and how much *should* the circumstances of the application of rights (as Tyulkina puts it, the political, social, legal, cultural, historical circumstances) matter in rights jurisprudence. As we have seen from Salát's article, circumstances present during the initialisation of the case can, do and *should* matter (the arguing for nuance and detail is after all what legal argumentation is partially about), but *should* the circumstances of application matter? The answer to that question might just give you the answer to the question of whether one is a "pluralist" or a "de-fragmentationalist".

Acknowledgements

This article was presented as part of a workshop funded by the MultiRights project. I wish to thank the participants to the workshop "Fragmentation of International Human Rights – Beyond the Conflict of Laws" held at the Central European University in Budapest which was funded by MultiRights project which is an advanced grant of the European Research Council – Lucas Lixinski, Svetlana Tylkina, Orsolya Salát, Kristin Henrard, Andreas Føllesdal, and Renata Uitz for helpful and lively discussion. I would also like to thank the Board and the reviewers of this journal for their comments; they were very helpful. And last, but not least, I wish to thank Natasha Telson for her Herculean efforts in facilitating the coordination of the whole issue.

Notes

1. B Simma and D Pulkowski, "Of Planets and the Universe: Self-contained Regimes in International Law" (2006) 17(3) *European J of Int Law* 483–529.
2. PM Dupuy, "A Doctrinal Debate in the Globalisation Era: On the 'Fragmentation' of International Law" (2007) 1 *European J of Legal Studies* 1–19.
3. B Simma and D Pulkowski, "Of Planets and the Universe: Self-contained Regimes in International Law" (2006) 17(3) *European J of Int Law* 483–529.

4. M Koskenniemi and P Leino, "Fragmentation of International Law? Postmodern Anxieties" (2002) 15(3) *Leiden J of Int Law* 553–79.
5. M Koskenniemi, *Report on Fragmentation of International Law: Difficulties Arising from the Diversification and Expansion of International Law* (Geneva, International Law Comm, 2006); MA Young. "Introduction: The Productive Friction Between Regimes", in MA Young (ed), *Regime Interaction in International Law: Facing Fragmentation* (Cambridge UP, Cambridge, 2011), at 5.
6. M Koskenniemi, *Report on Fragmentation of International Law: Difficulties Arising from the Diversification and Expansion of International Law* (Geneva, International Law Comm, 2006).
7. Case T–85/09, *Kadi v Commission*, [2010] ECR II–5177.
8. Case C–402/05 P and C–415/05, *P. Kadi & Al Barakaat International Foundation v Council & Commission*, [2008] ECR I–6351.
9. M Koskenniemi, *Report on Fragmentation of International Law: Difficulties Arising from the Diversification and Expansion of International Law* (Geneva, International Law Comm, 2006).
10. http://www.freakonomics.com/2009/09/17/survivor-bias-on-the-gridiron/ (last accessed 1 October 2013).
11. Example taken from http://youarenotsosmart.com/2013/05/23/survivorship-bias/ (last accessed 1 October 2013).
12. J Crawford and P Nevill, "Relations between International Courts and Tribunals: The 'Regime Problem'", in M Young (ed), *Regime Interaction in International Law* (Cambridge UP, Cambridge, 2012).
13. M Koskenniemi, *Report on Fragmentation of International Law: Difficulties Arising from the Diversification and Expansion of International Law* (Geneva, International Law Comm, 2006).
14. T Broude and Y Shany (eds), *Multi-Sourced Equivalent Norms in International Law* (Studies in International Law, Hart Publishing, Oxford, Portland OR, 2011).
15. T Broude and Y Shany (eds), *Multi-Sourced Equivalent Norms in International Law* (Studies in International Law, Hart Publishing, Oxford, Portland OR, 2011); but also see F Fontanelli, Review of "Tomer Broude and Yuval Shany (eds). Multi-Sourced Equivalent Norms in International Law" (2012) 23(2) *European J of Int Law* 597–604.
16. P Webb, *International Judicial Integration and Fragmentation* (Oxford UP, Oxford, 2013).
17. See, for example, the Preambles of the European Convention on Human Rights, the American Convention on Human Rights, the International Covenant on Civil and Political Rights, the International Covenant on Economic, Social and Cultural Rights, the UN Convention on the Rights of the Child, which in different ways credit the Universal Declaration on Human Rights.
18. Here I use the expression "by most similar cases" as it is most widely used in social sciences to denote case selection rather than its legal studies counterpart to denote individual cases decided by a panel of judges. In this sense, in this sentence, the words "cases" and "case selection" mean the three jurisdictions that are under scrutiny in this study as subjects of study, and not their jurisprudence. Throughout this introduction and in the studies themselves, cases, case-law or similar phrases are used in their more common legal studies meaning rather than their sociological meaning. See for instance Chapters 2 and 3 of S Choudhry, *The Migration of Constitutional Ideas* (Cambridge UP, Cambridge, 2006).
19. *Unn & Ben Leirvag v Norway*, Comm No 1155/2003, HRC, UN Doc CCPR/C/82/D/1155/2003, 23 November 2004; and ECtHR, *Folgero v Norway*, App No 15472/02, Judgment of 29 June 2007; but also see L Lixinski, "Choice of Forum in International Human Rights Adjudication and the Unity/Fragmentation Debate: Is Plurality the Way Forward?" (2008) XVIII *Italian Yearbook of International Law* 183–200.
20. M Koskenniemi, "Hegemonic Regimes", in M Young (ed), *Regime Interaction in International Law: Facing Fragmentation* (Cambridge UP, Cambridge, 2011), 305–24.
21. European Convention of Human Rights, art 3; International Covenant on Civil and Political Rights, art 7; American Convention on Human Rights, art 5.
22. For a key international law proponent of this stream of thought see M Koskenniemi, "Letter to the Editors of the Symposium" (1999) 93(2) *American J of Int Law* 351–61; M Koskenniemi, *From Apology to Utopia: the Structure of International Legal Argument: Reissue with a New Epilogue* (Cambridge UP, Cambridge, 2005); M Koskenniemi, *The Politics of International Law* (Oxford; Portland, OR, Hart Publishing, 2011).
23. It is arguable how much "choice" is really involved in interpreting one way rather than another since some, myself included, who argue the indeterminacy thesis also claim that in the end what

settles indeterminacy is the substantive notion – a substantive worldview – in which we are convinced and through which texts, sentences, paintings, utterances make sense. If that is the case then we also have to accept that we do not exactly control which worldviews we are persuaded and convinced in and therefore have no "choice" but to interpret texts one way rather than another; see for instance: S Fish, "Working on the Chain Gang: Interpretation in the Law and in Literary Criticism" (1982) 9(1) *Critical Inquiry* 201–16; S Fish, "Wrong Again" (1983) 62 *Texas Law Rev* 229–316; S Fish, "Still Wrong after All These Years" (1987) 6(3) *Law and Philosophy* 401–18; S Fish, *Doing What Comes Naturally: Change, Rhetoric, and the Practice of Theory in Literary and Legal Studies* (Duke UP, Durham NC, 1989), especially the chapter titled *Change* (141–59).

24. M Koskenniemi, *The Politics of International Law* (Oxford; Portland, OR, Hart Publishing, 2011).
25. The idea of "interpretative communities" has been championed by Stanley Fish, his most detailed explication of his concept can be found in S Fish, *Is there a Text in this Class?: The Authority of Interpretive Communities* (Harvard UP, Cambridge MA, 1980); S Fish, *Doing What Comes Naturally: Change, Rhetoric, and the Practice of Theory in Literary and Legal Studies* (Duke UP, Durham NC, 1989); S Fish "Afterword", in GA Olson and L Worsham (eds), *Postmodern Sophistry: Stanley Fish and the Critical Enterprise* (State U of New York P, Albany, 2004), 273–84.
26. S Fish, "Working on the Chain Gang: Interpretation in the Law and in Literary Criticism" (1982) 9(1) *Critical Inquiry* 201–16; S Fish, "Wrong Again" (1983) 62 *Texas Law Rev* 229–316; S Fish, "Still Wrong after All These Years" (1987) 6(3) *Law and Philosophy* 401–18.
27. As of 7 June 2013.
28. E Voeten, "The Impartiality of International Judges: Evidence from the European Court of Human Rights" (2008) 102(4) *American Pol Sci Rev* 417–33; Y Lupu and E Voeten, "Precedent in International Courts: A Network Analysis of Case Citations by the European Court of Human Rights" (2012) 42(2) *British Journal of Political Science* 413–39.
29. For the methodology and coding please visit http://dvn.iq.harvard.edu/dvn/dv/Voeten/faces/study/StudyPage.xhtml?globalId=hdl:1902.1/19324&studyListingIndex=0_9c0f66c3d256529f67040b4a858d (last visited 7 June 2013).
30. N Krisch, *Beyond Constitutionalism: The Pluralist Structure of Postnational Law* (Oxford UP, Oxford, New York, 2010).
31. M Koskenniemi, "Hegemonic Regimes", in M Young (ed), *Regime Interaction in International Law: Facing Fragmentation* (Cambridge UP, Cambridge, 2011), 305–24.
32. O Salát, "Comparative Freedom of Assembly and the Fragmentation of International Human Rights Law" (2014) 32(2) *Nordic Journal of Human Rights* 140–156.
33. S Tyulkina, "Fragmentation in International Human Rights Law: Political Parties and Freedom of Association in the Practice of the UN Human Rights Committee, European Court of Human Rights and Inter-American Court of Human Rights" (2014) 32(2) *Nordic Journal of Human Rights* 157–175.
34. M de S-O l'E Lasser, "The European Pasteurization of French Law" (2004) 90 *Cornell L Rev* 995; M de S-O l'E Lasser, *Judicial Transformations: The Rights Revolution in the Courts of Europe* (Oxford UP, Oxford, New York 2009).
35. *Lautsi v Italy*, Application No 30814/06, ECtHR, Grand Chamber, 18 March 2011.
36. P Ronchi, "Crucifixes, Margin of Appreciation and Consensus: The Grand Chamber Ruling in Lautsi v Italy" (2011) 13(3) *Ecclesiastical Law J* 287–97.

Comparative International Human Rights Law: An Analysis of the Right to Private and Family Life across Human Rights "Jurisdictions"

Lucas Lixinski

This article compares the application of the right to private and family life across different human rights jurisdictions. It chooses instances of "convergence" (that is, situations that fall under the purview of this right for all jurisdictions) and of "divergence" (situations that fall under the right for some jurisdictions, but under a different right in others). Through this exercise, the article demonstrates how the similarity in the language of the relevant treaties influences treaty application for the "easy" cases, but how, when faced with a "hard" case, a human rights jurisdiction is more likely to follow its own path, which is often more attuned to the legal sensitivities around the implementing body. Therefore, while at the same time institutional fragmentation is avoided in the instances of convergence, the hegemonic tendencies of international human rights law as a European project are also skirted, as seen in the "divergence" cases.

I. Introduction

Words like "fragmentation" and "constitutionalisation" are now commonplace in the international lawyer's vocabulary. A fair amount of ink and server space has been devoted to publishing papers considering these two closely related phenomena.[1] Some of that attention has been devoted to the specific field of human rights, and this article (and the Special Issue in which it is inserted) adds to that. More specifically, this contribution deals with how different human rights (quasi-)adjudicatory bodies have dealt with the same right across their different bodies.

One noteworthy characteristic of this experiment in constitutionalisation/fragmentation is that general human rights instruments share very similar language for the substantive provisions protecting each given right, dating back to the Universal Declaration of Human Rights (UDHR).[2] In other words, all of these instruments will protect, say, the right to freedom of expression, and will use fairly similar language to do so.

These similarities in language arise largely from the fact that the drafting of each instrument necessarily takes into account, and often builds on, the language of previous instruments. In this sense, and to use only a few UN-era examples, the European Convention on Human Rights (ECHR)[3] of 1950 built on the UDHR (1948), the International Covenant on Civil and Political Rights (ICCPR)[4] of 1966 built on the ECHR, the American Convention on Human Rights (ACHR)[5] of 1969 built on the ICCPR, and the African Charter of Human and Peoples' Rights (ACHPR)[6] of 1981 built on all of its predecessors.

Naturally, there is substantial variation across these instruments, which take into account the political necessities of their day, regional specificities, as well as the limits of the institutional framework within which they are to operate (both in terms of constitutional limitations and the willingness of participating states). This is even more pronounced when it comes to regional instruments like the ECHR and ACHR.

However, most of the variation is restricted to the bureaucratic and institutional apparatuses created by each of these instruments. When it comes to the language of the substantive rights, the similarities are striking. This, it seems, can be traced back to the notion of universalism of international human rights norms. Out of the instruments analysed here, nowhere is this universality most challenged than in the Banjul Charter, because of its introduction of the notion of (and chapter on) peoples' rights. However, when it comes to individual rights, the language is still fairly similar to previous instruments.

Has the similarity in language led to the virtually uniform application of these rights, in terms of tests and the range of situations covered by the right? Or, rather, has the small amount of variation (and/or external factors) led to differing interpretations and applications of these roughly identical rights? More importantly, what does the identity (or variance) mean for the international human rights project/system at large?

These are some of the questions to be explored. I will use the right to private and family life, as applied by international human rights (quasi-)adjudicatory bodies, as a case study. That is because it is a fairly fluid and open-ended right, which has been used as a blanket clause in the adjudication of many varied areas that were not originally thought of as falling under international human rights law. Because of this elasticity, and constant renewal of sorts of the right, the right can serve as a good ground upon which to analyse the elasticity of human rights more generally, and the way international human rights law responds to external pressures, be they from other areas of international law, or from other jurisprudential bodies within the same area.

This article will focus on certain specific areas of the adjudication of this right which present what I consider to be the best opportunities for comparing and contrasting the implementation of the right to family life. The cases discussed here under each chosen topic reflect both the leading cases and the current state of the jurisprudence at the time of writing. I believe that, while selective due to word constraints, the cases displayed here also present a fairly accurate depiction of the broader landscape of the international adjudication of the right to family life.

This contribution will not look at the African system, because of its relatively underdeveloped case-law, and will instead focus on the systems created by the ECHR, ICCPR, and ACHR. The article will proceed as follows: the next section will discuss the notion of comparing international human rights standards in the abstract, setting the scene for the third section, which will focus on the right to private and family life. There, I shall look at two different examples: one of convergence, and one of divergence. The fourth section will attempt to extrapolate some of these ideas beyond the realm of international human rights law, re-engaging with the notions of fragmentation and constitutionalisation of international law. The fifth section concludes the article.

II. Comparative International Human Rights Standards

Certainly, of all areas of international law, international human rights is one of the most-often connected to constitutionalist narratives of the international legal order. It is also, however, one of the least theorised in that context. Scholars like Mattias Kumm[7] have attempted to bridge this gap. His idea of "cosmopolitan constitutionalism" relies on human rights as a fundamental normative aspiration of a constitutionalised international legal order,

Table 1

ECHR, article 8	ICCPR, article 17	ACHR, article 11	American Declaration
1. Everyone has the right to respect for his private and family life, his home and his correspondence. 2. There shall be no interference by a public authority with the exercise of this right except such as is in accordance with the law and is necessary in a democratic society in the interests of national security, public safety or the economic well-being of the country, for the prevention of disorder or crime, for the protection of health or morals, or for the protection of the rights and freedoms of others.	1. No one shall be subjected to arbitrary or unlawful interference with his privacy, family, home or correspondence, nor to unlawful attacks on his honor and reputation. 2. Everyone has the right to the protection of the law against such interference or attacks.	1. Everyone has the right to have his honor respected and his dignity recognised. 2. No one may be the object of arbitrary or abusive interference with his private life, his family, his home, or his correspondence, or of unlawful attacks on his honor or reputation. 3. Everyone has the right to the protection of the law against such interference or attacks.	Article V [Right to protection of honor, personal reputation, and private and family life]. Every person has the right to the protection of the law against abusive attacks upon his honor, his reputation, and his private and family life....Article IX [Right to inviolability of the home]. Every person has the right to the inviolability of his home. Article X [Right to the inviolability and transmission of correspondence]. Every person has the right to the inviolability and transmission of his correspondence.

IV. Case-law Convergences

Perhaps the biggest similarity across these regimes is that they all subject the right to private and family life to a proportionality test when assessing alleged violations of it. There is also a commonly shared assumption across all three systems that this right entails both negative and positive obligations. However, there is also much convergence in the types of situations covered by the right to private and family life. For instance, all three systems have understood that the right applies to situations of home searches,[23] reputation issues,[24] treatment of prisoners,[25] surveillance,[26] and reproductive rights.[27]

The cases on treatment of prisoners are particularly helpful to our analysis, as all three bodies have dealt with cases involving the violation of prisoners' correspondence. For instance, in *Biscet v Cuba (Case 12.476)* (2007),[28] a case decided by the Inter-American Commission with respect to the American Declaration (because Cuba is not a party to the ACHR), the Commission was asked to assess the rights of political prisoners with respect to their communications with the outside world.

The case was about a 2003 crack-down against a number of human rights activists and independent journalists in Cuba, resulting in a number of arrests.[29] These individuals were engaged in activities such as publishing opinion pieces on Cuban social and economic matters, participating in groups that the authorities considered "counter-revolutionary" or as having contact with individuals considered "hostile" to Cuban government interests.[30] The petitioners were held in prisons far from their places of residence so as to make it difficult for family members to visit.[31] The Commission observed that the state has not provided any contrary evidence to the petitioners, and that the claims were corroborated by other sources. It therefore accepted the facts alleged on the basis of Rules of Procedure, article 39 that a petition's claims are presumed true if the state does not provide "responsive information" to them.[32]

In relation to article V (right to protection of honour, personal reputation, and private and family life), the Commission found a violation because some victims had been targets of "*actos de repudio*" (acts of repudiation or censure), which involved "insults, harassment and threats by State agents against those who oppose the government and are staged in the presence of family members, friends or colleagues. The purpose of these *actos de repudio* is to publicise the names and addresses of the alleged victims, branding them as counter-revolutionaries and encouraging other citizens to disown them and even fight them". In relation to those victims, a violation of article V was shown, because of the damage to their reputation.[33] And, specifically with respect to article X (inviolability and transmission of correspondence), the Commission noted that Cuba "has withheld or intercepted the correspondence and telephone communications between some of the victims and their relatives or attorneys". Thus, a violation of the inviolability of correspondence was shown.[34] Importantly, though, the Commission did not engage in a proportionality analysis in this case. Yet that, I suggest, can be attributed to the fact that Cuba did not present a defence at any stage, which allowed the Commission to turn any interference with the relevant right directly into a violation

Another relevant lesson from this case can be found in the preliminary considerations issued by the Commission. More specifically, the Commission considered its position in the field of international human rights law, and what that meant in its legal determinations:

> 41. In accordance with the jurisprudence of the inter-American human rights system, the provisions of its instruments, including the American Declaration, should be interpreted and applied within the context of the inter-American and international human rights systems and, in

the broader sense, in the light of the evolution of international human rights law. Thus, when examining a petition ... the Commission must pay attention to the other relevant norms of international law that apply to the member States and to the evolution of the *corpus juris gentium* of international human rights law over the course of time.

42. In particular, ... the evolution of the body of international human rights law relevant to the interpretation and application of the American Declaration can be extracted from other international and regional instruments on human rights. This includes the American Convention ... and its respective protocols ... [as well as] other multilateral agreements approved both within and outside the inter-American system ...

43. In its analysis of the instant case, the Commission will interpret and apply the relevant provisions of the American Declaration – as appropriate – in light of the evolution that international law of human rights has undergone, as set out in the treaties, custom, and other relevant sources of international law. (footnotes omitted)

This case thus seems to suggest that, when faced with a difficult situation (here, a non-cooperating state), bodies may feel the need to make stronger statements about their legitimacy, and, at least in this case, reliance on other bodies and instruments is seen as a means to enhance such legitimacy. Further, because all of these instruments, in a way, derive from the same "*corpus iuris gentium*",[35] it is possible and sometimes desirable to treat them as mutually reinforcing norms.

Despite not being able to fully develop the test with respect to the right to private and family life in this case, the bodies of the Inter-American system had the chance to fully flesh out their approach to article 11 in other cases. For instance, in *Escher v Brazil*,[36] involving wiretapping, the court determined that the right protected in article 11 was subject to restrictions "required by law, in pursuance of a legitimate objective, and required in a democratic society".[37] It is noteworthy that this language is nowhere to be found in the text of the American Convention, but is very close to that contained in ECHR, article 8(2). In undertaking this analysis, after determining there had been an interference with the right, the court found that said interference was not required by law, and that, therefore, a violation of article 11 had been established without the need to decide whether the object was legitimate, and was required in a democratic society. Even though this case stopped at the finding that the interference was not required by law, the test laid out by the Inter-American Court was remarkably similar to the way the European Court of Human Rights deals with article 8 cases.

In *Silver v United Kingdom*,[38] the European Court of Human Rights analysed the issue of restrictions on prisoner correspondence. In the case, seven prisoners complained of the interception of mail by prison authorities, having written to various organisations about their mistreatment in prison. The court followed its standard proportionality test. In deciding whether there had been an interference with the right, it said that the interception of the mail was an interference with the prisoners' right to respect for private life and the right to freedom of expression. It also determined that the interference was in accordance with the law, by noting that the prison authorities had acted pursuant to the Prison Act 1951 (Cth) and delegated legislation that was public, as well as administrative orders and instructions that were not made public. The court found that the Act and Rules with the administrative Orders and Instructions met the requirement that the law be "accessible", and that therefore the restriction was in accordance with the law. Finally, when determining whether it had been necessary, the court said that for several items of mail, concerning a prisoner's attempts to conduct suspicious business activities and letters threatening violence, the interception had indeed been necessary. Restrictions on the basis that the correspondence was with journalists, legal advisers, human rights bodies, or which discussed maltreatment or which attempted to stimulate public agitation or petition, were not "necessary". There was therefore a violation of article 8 with respect to some items of correspondence, but not others.

The Human Rights Committee, in *Estrella v Uruguay*, entertained the case of an Argentinian musician affiliated with the Peronista movement in Argentina, whose activities (including concerts and lectures) were considered subversive by the Uruguayan government, leading to his imprisonment and torture under the military dictatorship. This involved heavy censorship of his correspondence, including sentences being deleted from correspondence, and letters simply not being delivered. He indicated to the HRC that he signed for the receipt of letters he never actually saw. Uruguay responded to the petition only so as to contest its admissibility, not making any observations on the merits. After declaring the case admissible, and not having the allegations on the merits contested, the HRC found a violation of ICCPR, article 17, in conjunction with article 10(1) (on human treatment of detainees).[39]

Similar to the Cuban case before the Inter-American Commission, here the state did not contest, so the HRC did not have the chance to fully expound on its standards for violations of article 17. Unlike the Inter-American Commission in *Biscet*, which took the non-appearance of Cuba as a challenge to its legitimacy, that needed to be reasserted with a longer exposition about the law, here the Human Rights Committee restricted itself to a more formalistic approach, and simply took the state's default to mean a violation of the right.

In *van Hulst v The Netherlands*,[40] on the other hand, the Committee did so. In that case, the issue before the Committee was whether the interception and recording of the author's (a prisoner in the Dutch system) telephone calls with his lawyer (ATMM) constituted an unlawful or arbitrary interference with his privacy, in violation of article 17 of the Covenant.[41] After having determined that there was in fact an interference, and that it was required by law, the Committee went on to analyse the proportionality of the interference, recalling its General Comment No 16 and its previous case-law,[42] in stating that "the requirement of reasonableness implies that any interference with privacy must be proportionate to the end sought, and must be necessary in the circumstances of any given case".[43] It ultimately distinguished between conversations that Van Hulst held with ATMM in the capacity of his lawyer, and conversations held separately, and which were in fact tapped only because of an investigation that had separately been initiated against ATMM. Because those conversations were not covered by attorney-client privilege, its use in Dutch courts was not a violation of van Hulst's privacy.[44]

As we can see, all three systems have adopted very similar approaches to the right to privacy when it comes to correspondence and other communications. But the random sample of cases analysed here also shows important differences among the three systems. The Inter-American system, for instance, is still applying a comparatively less sophisticated instrument (the American Declaration) in some cases, which seems to spur it to seek support for its legitimacy in the case-law of other bodies, and other instruments (thereby reinforcing the notion of MSEN analysed in the previous section). Also, both the HRC and the Inter-American system face situations in which states simply refuse to engage with the relevant bodies, and cases are decided by default. Judgments by default are bad not only because they often hinder the development of the jurisprudence (even if this is our primary concern for the present purposes), but, most importantly, because they are harder to implement than an otherwise "normal" finding of a violation of international human rights. This difficulty is compounded also because the organs in the present examples (the HRC and the Inter-

American Commission) only have the power to issue recommendations, and not binding judgments.

V. Case-law Divergences

The case-law under each treaty has, in many instances, evolved in a similar direction. When it comes to the scope of situations that can be covered by the right to private and family life, it is clear that the ECHR is the one that has gone the furthest in turning its provision on private and family life into a blanket clause, by concluding that the notion of "private and family life" can include anything that interferes with the lives, lifestyle and livelihood of involved persons (as long as it is not already clearly covered by another right, presumably). The HRC, IACmHR and IACtHR have been somewhat more cautious in expanding this right, and have instead relied on other provisions as their go-to blanket clauses (the right to life is one that comes to mind for both instruments,[45] but also the general provision on the enjoyment of rights contained in the ACHR).[46]

Subject matters which only one or two of the systems have considered to fall under the right to private and family life include domestic violence (ECtHR),[47] housing (ECtHR and IACtHR),[48] enforced disappearances (IACtHR),[49] indigenous and minority rights (ECtHR and HRC),[50] sexual freedom (ECtHR and HRC),[51] environmental rights (ECtHR),[52] and migration (IACmHR and HRC),[53] among others.

Out of these, environmental rights could be an interesting point of analysis. The dominant approach among international environmental lawyers nowadays seems to be an ecocentric one, that is, an approach that justifies environmental protection as a goal in itself, being the environment worthy of protection not because it is important for human beings, but because it possesses an intrinsic value. An anthropocentric approach, that was the dominant one for several decades, advocates the importance of the environment in terms of what it represents for human beings.[54]

There are basically two ways in which human rights and the environment interact: the first one is by allowing limitations to the exercise of certain human rights for the sake of environmental protection; the second one, and the focus of the available case-law, is the "environmental content" of certain human rights, or rather how certain human rights are open enough in their content to allow for environmental considerations.

The European Court of Human Rights has dealt with the issue of environmental protection in several cases, always connecting them to the right to private and family life. The first one of them, *López Ostra v Spain*,[55] has set the bar for the case-law on the connection between human rights and the environment in this court.

Mrs Gregoria Lopez Ostra lived in the vicinities of several leather industries, who produced a great amount of waste that was dumped into the nearby river, causing an excessive amount of pollution that brought nausea and several other health problems to people exposed to it.[56] The Commission presented the case alleging a violation of articles 3 (cruel, inhuman and degrading treatment) and 8 (private and family life) of the European Convention.[57]

When analysing the case under article 8, the court established that "a *certain* margin of appreciation" (as opposed to a "wide" margin of appreciation) was left to states in the application of environmental policies, and that it was not important to determine whether the obligations in this case were positive or negative.[58] However, when it came to the application of these principles to the facts, the court said it only would analyse whether the national authorities had taken the necessary measures to protect the right to private and family life of Mrs López and her family,[59] which brings the case to an assessment of positive obligations, a view confirmed by the lack of a proportionality analysis of any interference. The court declared a violation of article 8[60] and, with respect to article 3, said that, even though the conditions to which the applicant had been submitted were certainly harsh, they did not amount to degrading treatment.[61]

Another relevant case is *Fadeyeva v Russia*, concerning the pollution caused by an iron smelter.[62] The court, when analysing the claims under article 8, stated that "no right to nature preservation is as such included among the rights and freedoms guaranteed by the Convention",[63] which can be read to mean that environmental concerns will only be relevant to the court insofar as they affect human lives, thus reaffirming the anthropocentric approach to environmentalism I argue to be necessary to human rights adjudication.

The ECtHR said that it was necessary to prove there had been an actual interference with the applicant's private life, and that this interference had been of a certain severity, to justify declaring a violation of article 8.[64] In doing such assessment, while concluding that the interference had not been directly caused by the state, the court found that its positive obligations connected the state to the interference.[65] And, even though this case was one of positive obligations, the court went on to analyse the proportionality of the interference, and it found that, despite the margin of appreciation granted to states for environmental matters (which even seemed to amount to deferentialism at some point),[66] the interference had been of such gravity so as to violate rights under article 8.[67]

This case means that a wide margin of appreciation is given to states in implementing their environmental policies, and that a proportionality analysis is required. This heightened burden might imply a certain unwillingness by the ECtHR to keep extending its jurisdiction into environmental law. At the same time, the extended margin of appreciation is consonant with the argument that environmental law usually opens more room for the reserved sovereign domain of states than human rights law. The fact that the ECtHR seems reluctant to take new environmental cases in, and the high degree of deference paid to national authorities in *Isayeva* might indicate a trend contrary to the expansion of jurisdiction into this area. It is hard to retreat from this expansion totally, though, once the court already has precedents on it. The next case, an earlier decision, does not take much of this approach into account, and offers a view more in favour of the expansion of jurisdiction.

In *Guerra v Italy*, the court analysed whether the lack of information about the polluting activities of a chemical factory amounted to a violation of rights protected under articles 10 (freedom of expression), 8 (right to private and family life) and 2 (right to life) of the ECHR.[68] Procedurally, it is important to mention that it was not the applicants, but rather the Commission, who invoked article 8: the applicants focused their case on article 10 and the right to receive information.[69] Subsequently the applicants linked the lack of access to information to a violation of their rights protected under articles 2 and 8,[70] and the court, in applying the principle of *jura novit curia*, decided it had jurisdiction *ratione materiae* to analyse the claims under all three articles of the ECHR.[71]

The claim under article 10 was dismissed for falling beyond the scope of the case.[72] When analysing the claim under article 8, the ECtHR affirmed that, since there had been no interference with the right, but rather the lack of compliance with a positive obligation, it would not undertake a proportionality analysis in the case.[73] And, when balancing the effect of the state's omission, it concluded there had been a breach of article 8.[74]

As to the claim on the right to life, the court decided that, since it had already declared a violation of article 8, it was not necessary to analyse the case under article 2 as well.[75] However, concurring opinions on the case expressed the view that there was a linkage between environmental concerns and the right to life,[76] which is actually how the HRC has addressed environmental human rights.

It is finally worth mentioning the *Hatton* case, which concerns noise pollution caused by night flights at Heathrow airport. The ECtHR in its first judgment said it made no difference whether the case was about a positive obligation or a direct interference, and that the proportionality test would be "broadly similar".[77] Additionally, the court initially found there had been a violation of the applicants' right to private and family life, citing the government's lack of measurement of the economic benefits of night flights as one of the reasons why the community gains could not be balanced against the harm suffered by those individuals.[78] However, the Grand Chamber of the ECtHR found differently. While admitting that the economic benefits had indeed not been measured, it asserted that not all aspects of the decision-making process in environmental matters need to be assessed, and that the applicants had been given a procedural opportunity to make a representation when the relevant scheme allowing night flights was being devised, which they ultimately did not take. Had this procedural opportunity been denied, there would have been stronger grounds for finding a violation of article 8, which, the Grand Chamber found, did not occur in the case.[79]

Following this case, the European Court has widened the scope of states' margin of appreciation also with respect to procedural aspects of environmental harm to individuals. Relevant for our present purposes, though, it still means that environmental matters fall under the right to private and family life in the European system, differently from the Human Rights Committee.

The three cases brought before the Human Rights Committee on environmental claims have all been declared inadmissible, on different grounds. Even so, while the HRC has never pronounced itself on the merits of the connection between the environmental and human rights, it has recognised some important links.

In *Port Hope Environmental Group v Canada*, for example, the HRC was asked to analyse whether the disposal of nuclear waste affected the right to life of present and future generations.[80] The Committee stated that the communication raised serious concerns with regard to the protection of the right to life under the ICCPR.[81] However, it understood that (1) the interests of future generations were to be treated only as an expression of concern to put the importance of the environmental matter "into due perspective";[82] and (2) that local remedies had not been exhausted,[83] thus declaring the communication inadmissible.[84]

Similarly, in *Susila Malani Dahanayake v Sri Lanka*, the Committee looked at a claim based on the right to life (ICCPR, article 6).[85] This case concerned the loss of livelihood and the harm caused to wetlands in Sri Lanka due to the construction of a road.[86] While the state recognised the link between the right to life and environmental protection,[87] and the HRC did not openly discard such connection, the Committee considered that the claim had not been significantly substantiated for the purposes of admissibility, and declared the communication inadmissible.[88]

Another case, *André Brun v France*, asked the Committee to look at the impact of Genetically Modified Organisms (GMOs) on the environment, based on the precautionary principle.[89] The author of the communication suggested initially a violation of the right to private and family life, in cross-fertilisation with the jurisprudence of the ECtHR,[90] and at a later stage suggested also the connection with the right to life, even citing the *Port Hope Environmental Group* case.[91] However, the Committee understood that a claim based on the precautionary principle could not be substantiated, as it was not an imminent threat of violation or an actual violation of any rights,[92] thus, the communication was declared inadmissible.[93] By rejecting a claim based on the precautionary principle, while not discarding the possibility of analysing cases based on actual environmental harm, the HRC seems to have determined the limits to which it would be willing to take jurisdiction with respect to environmental claims.

The Inter-American system has a unique approach to environmental issues, and tends to connect the protection of the environment with the protection of indigeneity.[94] Most cases brought before either one of these bodies involving environmental harms concern indigenous communities, and one of these cases gets to the point of categorising the effects of pollution into material values (including health) and the spiritual values associated with the environment.[95]

This case, involving the Community of San Mateo de Huanchor in Peru, concerns the pollution caused by a toxic waste sludge next to the community,[96] and a claim to the violation of the right to life, among others,[97] has been declared admissible by the Inter-American Commission.[98] It is important to mention that, while the petitioners also claimed a violation of the right to the protection of dignity and the right to protection of the family, these claims have been deemed unfounded by the Commission, and will not be analysed on their merits.[99] This means that, while the Commission accepts the connection between the right to life and the environment, it seems to reject the connection with private and family life, characteristic of the European system.

Another case, involving the effects of the construction of a dam in Chile, did not frame the connection between indigenous peoples and the environment based on the right to life, but rather on the right to physical integrity and the right to freedom of religion,[100] thus reinforcing the connection between the spiritual element of indigeneity and the environment characteristic of the Inter-American system. The case ended in a friendly settlement, however, and the Commission did not have the opportunity to analyse the merits of such connection.

The *Case of the Saramaka Community v Suriname* is also an important example of an environmental claim that has not been fully recognised within the case itself. In this case, the claims for human rights violations deriving from the environmental harm caused by a mining project on indigenous lands were rejected by the court in the Preliminary Objections phase. The Commission did not present the environmental claim in its original petition and, even though the representatives are able to present new legal claims before the court in any given case, they must do so within the set of facts as presented by the Commission. The Commission failed in its initial petition to mention the environmental harm caused by the mining project, and thus the claim was rejected by the court.[101] This would have been a great opportunity for the court to directly address the human rights dimension of pollution, but it failed on procedural grounds.

In *Kawas Fernández v Honduras*, the court analysed the violation of the right to freedom of association of an environmental activist who had been murdered because of her activities. The claim was that the deprivation of her life had also brought with it the violation of her right to freely associate with others.[102] The court connected her work as an environmental activist to that of a human rights defender, putting environmental rights within the category of ESCR, as the Additional Protocol to the American Convention on Human Rights in the Area of Economic, Social and Cultural Rights ("Protocol of San Salvador") declares the right to a healthy environment in its article 11.[103] The court acknowledged the causal relationship between the murder of Jeanette Kawas Fernández by state agents and the interference with her right to freedom of association. It also mentioned the chilling effect that this interference had on other environmental activists.[104] Based on these factors, it declared there had been a violation by the state of the victim's freedom of association.[105]

One of the most recent decisions with respect to environmental issues, *Sarayaku v Ecuador*,[106] considered the issue of oil exploitation in indigenous lands. The case revolved more broadly around the issue of the free, prior and informed consent of the community with respect to oil exploitation, though, and did not fully consider the issue of a right to a healthy environment. It found a violation of the provision on property rights (ACHR, article 21) with respect to the community, because of the state's failure to consult them fully.[107] Even though the Inter-American Commission tried to make an argument connecting pollution to a violation of the right to life,[108] the court dismissed that argument, saying it would be unreasonable to expect the state to have a positive obligation in this instance (since the pollution was caused by a private party, and not the state directly).[109]

What these cases show us is that, despite many convergences, when it comes to "boundary-pushing" under their instruments, the three systems under analysis here take their own roads, and do not seem nearly as concerned with coordinating approaches. It is difficult to ascertain why different approaches have been taken (it could be simply because that is the way the complaints were brought before them by the alleged victims), but there is certainly something liberating about each body not feeling necessarily bound to and by the others. But what do these convergences and divergences mean, not only for international human rights law, but for international law more generally? The next section addresses this issue.

VI. Lessons beyond Human Rights?

Linguistic similarity in the provisions with respect to the right to private and family life leads to a certain degree of uniformity in the application of standards of review and their scope. That is because the language of most relevant instruments already contains the tests. Somewhat surprisingly, though, even where there is no language for a test in one of the instruments (the ICCPR), there is still application of the same standard as that of other instruments, so there is a fair amount of spillover. These degrees of identity and variation with respect to these provisions lead in effect to a stronger body of international human rights law, with some significant impacts beyond international human rights law.

This discussion on comparing the right to private and family life brings forth the issue of institutional fragmentation in international human rights law. Even if somewhat neglected in the ILC Report on Fragmentation,[110] it is an important dimension to be considered, and the specific context of international human rights law offers a particularly fertile ground for this analysis. This is so because, as discussed above, human rights language is fairly similar among the several instruments, so there is less to be said about the normative divergences or convergences of the system; convergence (to a certain minimum level) is in fact a given at the level of the language adopted by the instruments. What differs is the way the provisions have been interpreted by each body over time (the object of the preceding section), and that is more the role of institutions than of the applicable law.

Debates on the fragmentation of international law are therefore essential to understand the dynamics of comparative human rights law. What these dynamics make abundantly clear beyond the narrow scope of international human rights law is that institutional fragmentation matters, and that context inevitably influences the way international law is applied.

The counterpoint to this discussion has to do with the role of international human rights law in projects about the constitutionalisation of international law. Two features need to be highlighted here: the first is about the place of human rights in a constitutional telling of international law; the other is about perspectives in narrating the international legal order. Regarding the place of human rights, we have already discussed how international human rights law plays a role in a constitutionalised international legal order that is at once central and vague. However, when it comes to perspectives, the big question is whether international human rights law is a constitutional project on its own, or whether it is willing to be merely a piece in a larger puzzle. Based on the mandate limitations of these bodies, and their built-in tendency to think about human rights as the central theme of the international legal order, it seems that these bodies are prevented from thinking of themselves as a piece in a larger puzzle.[111] This notion suggests that they are bound to think of themselves as constitutional projects in their own right, a process that inevitably leads to fragmentation.[112]

Of course, fragmentation from above is only pluralism from below. So, in a way, international human rights bodies can in fact contribute to a more pluralistic legal order. In fact, by refusing to defer to one another openly, they are leaving the door open precisely for that pluralism, avoiding the hegemonic tendencies of the international human rights legal project.

In trying to bring this discussion to the realm of "general" international law, I would suggest that there are possibilities for greater normative integration in international law, but that these should be treated with caution, because of both the hegemonic tendencies of any such project, and also the related notion that harmonisation leads to disregarding regional specificities, be it a need for a system to affirm itself (like the Inter-American Commission) or the reluctance of parties to engage with systems they are parties to (as in the case of the Human Rights Committee). These regional specificities also come into play when the system is testing its own limits and therefore, when international law is attempting to cover gaps in international governance (so important for any constitutional telling of international law), one must take into account the fact that different regions will respond with very different means to address those gaps, and to challenge those differences might lead back to the same legitimacy problems. Cross-judicial dialogue comes a long way in helping bridge certain gaps, but its importance should not be over-estimated. While it is a valuable means to enhance a system's internal legitimacy, it is not necessarily used when a regime wants to expand itself, but does not feel its legitimacy is at risk.

VII. Concluding Remarks

Even though there are multiple fora to address individual cases with respect to human rights violations, applying a range of different instruments, fragmentation does not seem to be much of a risk for international human rights law. Part of that is an internalised notion of universality of international human rights law (tailored to a certain extent to local circumstances), and part of that is the more pragmatic fact that the text upon which the (quasi-)adjudicatory bodies are relying is virtually the same.

The right to private and family life, though, also shows another facet. For the most part, tests are very similar with respect to situations that clearly fall under the purview of this right. Much of that can be attributed to linguistic similarities, but the case of the ICCPR (which does not contain a limitations clause, but still applies a test nearly identical to that of instruments containing such a clause) is telling of a tendency to treat human rights law as a fairly uniform body of law, regardless of jurisdiction.

Nevertheless, the right to private and family life has also been used, to a smaller or larger extent, as a means to expand the range of situations covered by human rights instruments. In these newer instances, or borderline cases, the situation is different, as the content of the right to private and family life becomes hazier, and some systems will not use it to cover situations that would fall under this right in another system.

Do these dissonances point at some sort of fragmentation of international human rights law? Perhaps they do. But they also serve as a means to enhance the internal legitimacy of each human rights system, by clearly staking its autonomy with respect to other systems. In this way, the leeway each body has to diverge from the others in these borderline cases serves to counter accusations of hegemony, of human rights being an European project imposed upon the rest of the world. This could have been the case in the beginning, but now each system has gone its own way, and expanded according to its own particular circumstances.

This proliferation of rights needs to be further considered in its ripple effects, particularly politically. The law is somewhat limited in what it can show, and this comparative exercise, while foregrounding convergences and divergences, fails to articulate why they happen. A suggestion would be to remind us of the tension between universalism (convergences) and relativism (divergences), but even that seems to be something of a cop out. One needs to consider whether, and to what extent, these bodies are strategic players in the broader war theatre of international law, advancing their own agendas and views on the body of international human rights beyond their constitutive treaties, or if they are rather only rule followers, simply implementing these constitutive instruments, and occasionally enjoying fortuitous overlaps and convergences. The evidence would suggest the former, but it is still unclear what they are fighting for.

Acknowledgements

I am highly indebted to Guy Baldwin for his research assistance, and for the input of anonymous reviewers and audiences in Oslo and Budapest. All errors remain my own.

Notes

1. One particular instance is a recent issue of the *Erasmus Law Review*, entirely dedicated to the matter of "Narratives of the International Legal Order and Why They Matter". See 6(1) *Erasmus Law Rev* (www.erasmuslawreview.nl).
2. Universal Declaration of Human Rights, adopted and proclaimed by General Assembly resolution 217 A (III) of 10 December 1948.
3. Convention for the Protection of Human Rights and Fundamental Freedoms, CETS 005, opened for signature on 4 November 1950. Entry into force: 3 September 1953. States Parties as of September 2013: 47.
4. International Covenant on Civil and Political Rights, adopted and opened for signature, ratification and accession by General Assembly resolution 2200A (XXI) of 16 December 1966. Entry into force: 23 March 1976. States parties as of September 2013: 167.
5. American Convention on Human Rights "Pact of San José, Costa Rica". Adopted on 22 November 1969. Entry into force: 18 July 1978. States Parties as of September 2013: 23.
6. African (Banjul) Charter on Human and Peoples' Rights, Adopted 27 June 1981 by OAU Doc CAB/LEG/67/3 rev. 5. Entry into force 21 October 1986. States parties as of September 2013: 53.
7. M Kumm, "The Cosmopolitan Turn in Constitutionalism: On the Relationship between Constitutionalism in and beyond the State", in Jeffrey L Dunoff and Joel P Trachtman (eds), *Ruling the World: Constitutionalism, International Law, and Global Governance* (Cambridge UP, Cambridge, 2009), 258–324.
8. T Broude and Y Shany, "The International Law and Policy of Multi-Sourced Equivalent Norms", in T Broude and Y Shany (eds), *Multi-Sourced Equivalent Norms in International Law* (Hart Publishing, Oxford, 2011), 1–15, at 9.

9. T Broude and Y Shany, "The International Law and Policy of Multi-Sourced Equivalent Norms", in T Broude and Y Shany (eds), *Multi-Sourced Equivalent Norms in International Law* (Hart Publishing, Oxford, 2011), 1–15, at 11–12.
10. C Charters, "Multi-Sourced Equivalent Norms and the Legitimacy of Indigenous Peoples' Rights under International Law", in T Broude and Y Shany (eds), *Multi-Sourced Equivalent Norms in International Law* (Hart Publishing, Oxford, 2011), 289–320, at 289.
11. P-M Dupuy, "Some Reflections on Contemporary International Law and the Appeal to Universal Values: A Response to Martti Koskenniemi" (2005) 16(1) *European J of Int Law* 131–37.
12. MM Mutua, *Human Rights: A Political and Cultural Critique* (U of Pennsylvania P, Philadelphia, 2008).
13. M Koskenniemi, "Hegemonic Regimes", in Margaret A Young (ed), *Regime Interaction in International Law: Facing Fragmentation* (Cambridge UP, Cambridge, 2012), 305–24.
14. L Lixinski, "Choice of Forum in International Human Rights Adjudication and the Unity/ Fragmentation Debate: Is Plurality the Way Ahead?" (2008) 18 *Italian Yearbook of International Law* 183–200.
15. Human Rights Committee Comm No 1155/2003 *Unn & Ben Leirvag v Norway*, UN Doc CCPR/ C/82/D/1155/2003 (23 November 2004); and European Court of Human Rights *Folgero v Norway* (Application No 15472/02) (29 June 2007).
16. A-M Slaughter, *A New World Order* (Princeton UP, Princeton, 2005).
17. N Rajkovic, "'Global Law' and Governmentality: Reconceptualizing the 'Rule of Law' as Rule 'Through' Law" (2012) 18(1) *European J of Int Relations* 29–52.
18. The American Declaration, despite being a non-binding instrument, is still often used by the Inter-American Commission with respect to individual complaints arising from individuals against OAS member states who are not parties to the ACHR (as per article 20 of the Inter-American Commission's Statute). It is therefore a valid instrument for the adjudication of these rights.
19. Article 30. Scope of Restrictions. The restrictions that, pursuant to this Convention, may be placed on the enjoyment or exercise of the rights or freedoms recognized herein may not be applied except in accordance with laws enacted for reasons of general interest and in accordance with the purpose for which such restrictions have been established.
20. See generally UNGA Third Committee, 15th Session (1960): A/C.3/SR.1016, [17] (SU); A/C.3/ SR.1018, [11]–[12] (USA); A/C.3/SR.1019, [6] (GH), [11] (R), [18] & [44] (PI), [22] (LIB), [24] (SA), [27] (IND), [32] (U); A/C.3/SR.1020, [15] (R), [27] (U); A/C.3/SR.1021, [2] (YU), [4] (RI) (rejecting the "necessary in a democratic society" standard for a limitations clause, and therefore rejecting an explicit limitations clause altogether).
21. See generally UNGA Third Committee, 9th Session (1954) and 15th Session (1960): A/C.3/ SR.565, [17] (AF); A/C.3/SR.1022, [7] (GB), [13] (PI), [16] (P), [24] (IL); E/CZN.4/SR.1023, [18] (PL); E/CN.4/SR.1024, [4] (CDN); E/CN.4/SR.1025, [49] (IL) (discussing the issue of uniformity across articles other than article 17).
22. General Comment No 16: The right to respect of privacy, family, home and correspondence, and protection of honour and reputation (article 17), 04/08/1988, paras 3–4: "3. The term 'unlawful' means that no interference can take place except in cases envisaged by the law. Interference authorized by States can only take place on the basis of law, which itself must comply with the provisions, aims and objectives of the Covenant. 4. The expression 'arbitrary interference' is also relevant to the protection of the right provided for in article 17. In the Committee's view the expression 'arbitrary interference' can also extend to interference provided for under the law. The introduction of the concept of arbitrariness is intended to guarantee that even interference provided for by law should be in accordance with the provisions, aims and objectives of the Covenant and should be, in any event, reasonable in the particular circumstances."
23. For the HRC: Human Rights Committee, *van Alphen v The Netherlands*, Comm No 305/1988. Views of 23 July 1990; Human Rights Committee, *Yklymova v Turkmenistan*, Comm No 1460/ 2006. Views of 20 July 2009. For the IACmHR: IACmHR, *Hector Pérez Salazar v Peru (Case 10.562)*, Report No 43/97, published 19 February 1998. For the ECtHR: ECtHR, *Niemietz v Germany (Application 13710/88)*. Judgment of 16 December 1992.
24. For the HRC: Human Rights Committee, *Birindwa & Tshisekedi v Zaire*, Comm No 241 & 242/ 198. Views of 2 November 1989; Human Rights Committee, *Sayadi v Belgium*, Comm No 1472/ 2006. Views of 22 October 2008. For the IACtHR: IACtHR, *Gómez-Paquiyauri Brothers v Peru.*

Judgment of 8 July 2004. For the ECtHR: ECtHR, *Sanchez Cardenas v Norway (Application 12148/03)*. Judgment of 4 October 2007.

25. For the HRC: Human Rights Committee, *Estrella v Uruguay*, Comm No 74/1980. Views of 29 March 1983. For the IACmHR: IACmHR, *Biscet v Cuba (Case 12.476)*, Report No 67/06, published 21 October 2006. For the ECtHR: ECtHR, *Campbell & Fell v United Kingdom (Application 7878/77)*. Judgment of 28 June 1984.
26. For the HRC: Human Rights Committee, *van Hulst v The Netherlands*, Comm No 903/1999. Views of 1 November 2004. For the IACtHR: IACtHR, *Escher v Brazil*. Judgment of 6 July 2009. For the ECHR: ECtHR, *Malone v United Kingdom (Application 8691/79)*. Judgment of 2 August 1984.
27. For the HRC: Human Rights Committee, *KNLH v Peru*, Comm No 1153/2003. Views of 24 October 2005. For the IACtHR: IACtHR, *Artavel Murillo v Costa Rica*. Judgment of 28 November 2012. For the ECtHR: ECtHR, *Tysiac v Poland (Application 5410/03)*. Judgment of 20 March 2007.
28. IACmHR, *Biscet v Cuba (Case 12.476)*, Report No 67/06, published 21 October 2006.
29. *Biscet v Cuba (Case 12.476)*, at para 12.
30. *Biscet v Cuba (Case 12.476)*, at para 17.
31. *Biscet v Cuba (Case 12.476)*, at para 19.
32. *Biscet v Cuba (Case 12.476)*, at paras 46–47.
33. *Biscet v Cuba (Case 12.476)*, at paras 232–34.
34. *Biscet v Cuba (Case 12.476)*, at paras 241–43.
35. AAC Trindade, "International Law for Humankind: Towards a New *Ius Gentium*" (2005) *Recueil des Cours* 316 and 317.
36. IACtHR, *Escher v Brazil*. Judgment of 6 July 2009.
37. *Escher v Brazil*, at para 116. The element of "necessary in a democratic society", as specified in another case, means that the interference must be idoneous, necessary and proportional. See *Tristan Donoso v Panama*. Judgment of 27 January 2009, at para 56.
38. ECtHR, *Silver v United Kingdom (Application No 5947/72; 6205/73; 7052/75; 7061/75; 7107/75; 7113/75; 7136/75)*. Judgment of 25 March 1983.
39. *Silver v United Kingdom*, at para 10.
40. Human Rights Committee, *van Hulst v The Netherlands*, Comm No 903/1999. Views of 1 November 2004.
41. *van Hulst v The Netherlands*, at para 7.2.
42. Human Rights Committee, *Toonen v Australia*, Comm No 488/1992. Views of 31 March 1994.
43. *van Hulst v The Netherlands*, at para 7.6.
44. *van Hulst v The Netherlands*, at para 7.10.
45. See for instance, Human Rights Committee, *Port Hope Environmental Group v Canada*, Comm No 67/1980. Views of 27 October 1982, paras 1.2–1.3. IACmHR, *Community of San Mateo de Huanchor & its Members v Peru (Case 504/03)*. Admissibility Report No 69/04, published 15 October 2004, para 16.
46. Article 1. Obligation to Respect Rights. 1. The States Parties to this Convention undertake to respect the rights and freedoms recognized herein and to ensure to all persons subject to their jurisdiction the free and full exercise of those rights and freedoms, without any discrimination for reasons of race, color, sex, language, religion, political or other opinion, national or social origin, economic status, birth, or any other social condition.
47. For the ECtHR: ECtHR, *ES v Slovakia (Application 8227/04)*. Judgment of 15 September 2009.
48. For the IACtHR: IACtHR, *Case of the Ituango Massacres v Colombia*. Judgment of 1 July 2006. For the ECtHR: ECtHR, *Demades v Turkey (Application 16219/90)*. Judgment of 31 July 2003.
49. For the IACtHR: IACtHR, *Case of Gelman v Uruguay*. Judgment of 24 February 2011.
50. For the HRC: Human Rights Committee, *Francis Hopu & Tepoaitu Bessert v France*, Comm No 549/1993. Views of 29 December 1997. For the ECtHR: *Chapman v United Kingdom (Application 27238/95)*. Judgment of 18 January 2001.
51. For the HRC: Human Rights Committee, *Joslin v New Zealand*, Comm No 902/1999. Views of 17 July 2002. For the ECtHR: *Dudgeon v United Kingdom (Application 7525/76)*. Judgment of 22 October 1981.
52. For the ECtHR: ECtHR, *Case of López Ostra v Spain (Application No 16798/90)*. Judgment of 9 December 1994.

53. For the HRC: Human Rights Committee, *Winata v Australia*, Comm No 930/2000. Views of 26 July 2001; for the IACmHR: *Wayne Smith, Hugo Armendariz v United States (Case 12.562)*, Report No 81/10, published 12 July 2010.
54. MA Orellana, *Derechos Humanos y Ambiente: Desafíos para el Sistema Interamericano de Derechos Humanos* (http://www.ciel.org/Publications/Morellana_DDHH_Nov07.pdf, 2007). Council of Europe Parliamentary Assembly, *Environment and Human Rights Report* (2003).
55. ECtHR, *Case of López Ostra v Spain (Application No 16798/90)*. Judgment of 9 December 1994.
56. *Case of López Ostra v Spain*, at paras 7–9.
57. *Case of López Ostra v Spain*, at para 1.
58. *Case of López Ostra v Spain*, at para 51.
59. *Case of López Ostra v Spain*, at para 55.
60. *Case of López Ostra v Spain*, at para 58.
61. *Case of López Ostra v Spain*, at para 60.
62. ECtHR, *Case of Fadeyeva v Russia (Application No 55723)*. Judgment of 30 November 2005, at paras 10–18.
63. *Case of Fadeyeva v Russia*, at para 68.
64. *Case of Fadeyeva v Russia*, at para 70.
65. *Case of Fadeyeva v Russia*, at paras 89–92.
66. *Case of Fadeyeva v Russia*, at para 105.
67. *Case of Fadeyeva v Russia*, at para 134.
68. ECtHR, *Case of Guerra v Italy (Application No 116/1996/735/932)*. Judgment of 19 February 1998, at paras 12–18.
69. *Case of Guerra v Italy*, at para 40.
70. *Case of Guerra v Italy*, at para 41.
71. *Case of Guerra v Italy*, at paras 42–44.
72. *Case of Guerra v Italy*, at para 54.
73. *Case of Guerra v Italy*, at para 58.
74. *Case of Guerra v Italy*, at para 60.
75. *Case of Guerra v Italy*, at para 62.
76. See *Concurring Opinion of Judge Walsh*, and *Concurring Opinion of Judge Jambrek*.
77. ECtHR, *Case of Hatton v United Kingdom (Application No 36022/97)*. Judgment of 2 October 2001, at para 96.
78. *Case of Hatton v United Kingdom*, at paras 100–7.
79. *Case of Hatton v United Kingdom*, at paras 116–30.
80. Human Rights Committee, *Port Hope Environmental Group v Canada*, Comm No 67/1980. Views of 27 October 1982, paras 1.2–1.3.
81. *Port Hope Environmental Group v Canada*, at para 8.
82. *Port Hope Environmental Group v Canada*, at para 8.a.
83. *Port Hope Environmental Group v Canada*, at para 8.b.
84. *Port Hope Environmental Group v Canada*, at para 9.
85. Human Rights Committee, *Susila Malani Dahanayake v Sri Lanka*, Comm No 1331/2004. Views of 14 September 2006, para 3.2.
86. *Susila Malani Dahanayake v Sri Lanka*, at para 2.2.
87. *Susila Malani Dahanayake v Sri Lanka*, at para 4.7.
88. *Susila Malani Dahanayake v Sri Lanka*, at paras 6.4 and 7.
89. Human Rights Committee, *André Brun v France*, Comm No 1453/2006. Views of 23 November 2006, at para 2.1.
90. *André Brun v France*, at para 3.1.
91. *André Brun v France*, at paras 5.2 and 5.6.
92. *André Brun v France*, at para 6.3.
93. *André Brun v France*, at para 7.
94. L Lixinski, "Treaty Interpretation by the Inter-American Court of Human Rights: Expansionism at the Service of the Unity of International Law" (2010) 21(3) *European J of Int Law* 585–604.
95. IACmHR, *Community of San Mateo de Huanchor & its Members v Peru (Case 504/03)*, Admissibility Report No 69/04, published 15 October 2004, para 16.
96. *Community of San Mateo de Huanchor & its Members v Peru*, at para 1.

97. *Community of San Mateo de Huanchor & its Members v Peru*, at para 66. These other rights include the rights to personal security, the right of the child and judicial protection.
98. *Community of San Mateo de Huanchor & its Members v Peru*, at para 67.
99. *Community of San Mateo de Huanchor & its Members v Peru*, at para 66.
100. IACmHR, *Mercedes Julia Huenteao Beroiza v Chile (Case 4617/02)*, Friendly Settlement Report No 30/04, published 11 March 2004. The original petition illustrating this claim, along with other documents of the case, is available at the website of the Centre for International Environmental Law (CIEL), who was doing the litigation of the case. See Centre for International Environmental Law website, available at http://www.ciel.org (last accessed 30 September 2013).
101. IACtHR, *Case of the Saramaka People. v Suriname*. Judgment of 28 November 2007, at paras 11–17.
102. IACtHR, *Case of Kawas-Fernández v Honduras*. Judgment of 3 April 2009, para 140.
103. *Case of Kawas-Fernández v Honduras*, at paras 147–48.
104. *Case of Kawas-Fernández v Honduras*, at paras 152–53.
105. *Case of Kawas-Fernández v Honduras*, at para 155.
106. IACtHR, *Case of the Kichwa Indigenous People of Sarayaku v Ecuador*. Judgment of 27 June 1012.
107. *Case of the Kichwa Indigenous People of Sarayaku v Ecuador*, at para 232.
108. *Case of the Kichwa Indigenous People of Sarayaku v Ecuador*, at para 233.
109. *Case of the Kichwa Indigenous People of Sarayaku v Ecuador*, at para 245.
110. L Lixinski, "Choice of Forum in International Human Rights Adjudication and the Unity/ Fragmentation Debate: Is Plurality the Way Ahead?" (2008) 18 *Italian Yearbook of International Law* 183–200; MA Young, "Introduction: the productive friction between regimes", in Margaret A Young (ed), *Regime Interaction in International Law: Facing Fragmentation* (Cambridge UP, Cambridge, 2012), 1–19.
111. L Lixinski, "Treaty Interpretation by the Inter-American Court of Human Rights: Expansionism at the Service of the Unity of International Law" (2010) 21(3) *European J of Int Law* 585–604.
112. M Ajevski, "International Criminal Law and Constitutionalization: On Hegemonic Narratives in Progress" (2013) 6(1) *Erasmus Law Rev* 50–61.

Freedom of Speech as Related to Journalists in the ECtHR, IACtHR and the Human Rights Committee – a Study of Fragmentation

Marjan Ajevski

In its report on the fragmentation in international law, the ILC decided not to deal with the issue of institutional fragmentation – the fragmentation of international law brought on by the existence of different institutions dealing with norms that are "normatively equivalent". This is a study of institutional fragmentation within human rights law; specifically it is an attempt to gauge the extent of fragmentation through the case-law of three courts, the Inter-American Court of Human Rights, the European Court of Human Rights and the Human Rights Committee, focusing on freedom of speech as related to journalists. It compares the texts, scope, tests and justifications of the three human rights conventions and concludes that, at least in this narrow field, the fear of fragmentation is unwarranted, with a large caveat which pertains to the doctrine of the margin of appreciation as practiced by the ECtHR and its "slipperiness".

1. Introduction

In its report[1] on the fragmentation in international law, the International Law Commission decided not to deal with the issue of institutional fragmentation – the fragmentation of international law brought on by the existence of different institutions dealing with norms that are "normatively equivalent".[2] Nowhere is this more apparent than in the field of international human rights since, while it aspires to global relevance, it is populated by judicial or quasi-judicial institutions[3] that have, not only limited geographical, but sometimes different substantive scope. In terms of normatively equivalent norms, the norms that these courts are tasked with applying find their roots in the Universal Declaration on Human Rights[4] and their respective founding instruments dedicate themselves to enforcing them. Yet, in terms of human rights institutions, the multiplication of human rights courts, in effect, increases the fear of fragmentation exponentially, since every human rights court can, even unwittingly, challenge the other institutions' interpretations of human rights. Consequently, the aim of this article is to ascertain the extent to which these fears are justifiable and to determine to what extent there is fragmentation (albeit in a very narrow scope) in international human rights.

The narrow scope of this study is as follows: it covers freedom of speech as related to journalists and the media in three jurisdictions: the European Court of Human Rights (ECtHR), the Inter-American Court of Human Rights (IACtHR) and the United Nations

Human Rights Committee (HRC). It takes a particular comparative perspective by comparing the texts, scope, tests, justifications and, to a limited extent, outcomes within these three jurisdictions as they are related to journalists and the media. The reason for choosing this field is that it is one of the core understandings of freedom of expression and, due to the media's constant use of this right, there has been a high number of instances where the right is invoked. This, in turn, produces a high number of cases and, therefore, a mature doctrine of free speech related to the media has developed. The analysis presented in this study will be structured around the comparison of texts, scope, and tests and justifications.

There are some limitations to this study beyond the obvious one of its narrow scope, including that the bias in selection runs the possibility of missing issues that can be quite salient in other rights and, as the saying goes, not seeing the wood for the trees. Other limitations are somewhat more prosaic but, nevertheless, also relevant. One limitation that stands out is the lack of accessibility and usability in the jurisprudence of some of the courts, namely the HRC. It lacks any systematised database of jurisprudence, not all of the cases are available online, and there is hardly any way of searching them systematically. The situation is somewhat better with the IACtHR, whose judgments, at least as related to free speech, are publicly available and translated into English. The easiest database to work with is the ECtHR's; however, the sheer number of cases makes it a daunting task to research. The consequence of this is that not all of the cases may be covered in this study; however there are enough cases and secondary literature[5] to give a degree of confidence in the comparison. Another limitation to the study is that, to the extent that any findings are generalisable, they would only pertain to the other qualified rights in the three conventions in question. This is to a large extent due to the fact that the structure through which the reasoning process in freedom of expression is put is the proportionality test, which is not a factor when dealing with unqualified or absolute rights such as the prohibitions of torture and slavery.

The argument in the article is structured as follows. I start with the comparison of the convention texts (section 2) as presented in the conventions and continue with the comparison of scope (section 3), tests (section 4) and justifications (section 5) as they are practised and interpreted by the courts. I will then continue with an analysis of the role that tests and justifications have in stabilising the jurisprudential outcomes of these courts and argue that it precisely the shared techniques, as well as the substantive notions of the role and purpose of human rights in democracy that these courts use, that accounts for most of the overlapping jurisprudential outcomes.

II. The Convention Texts

The text of the conventions differ to some extent, either in their statement of principles in the preamble or in the text of the articles covering freedom of speech. Due to their historical development, some are far shorter than others, namely the European Convention, which only has two paragraphs in the article covering freedom of speech, while the American Convention and the Covenant have five and three, respectively. The preambles also show the particularities of the Conventions themselves, for instance the European Convention[6] and the American Convention[7] reference their regional character, while the Covenant[8] emphasises its attachment to the United Nations as a global organisation. However, all three[9] show a firm commitment to the Universal Declaration of Human Rights[10] and partially present themselves as its enforcement mechanism.

One other textual difference comes into view, regarding the preambles, that is relevant to the discussion regarding the justifications and tests later in this article, and that is that while the European and American Conventions prominently state that they represent a commitment of democratic nations to democracy[11], the Covenant almost shies away from the word, and mentions it only three times, in articles 14, 21 and 22 but not in article 19. On quick inspection, there seems to be no logical reason why the term "necessary in a democratic society" would not be included in article 19 while being included in articles 21 and 22 (freedoms of assembly and association, respectively). It is not as though the articles themselves deal with unrelated matters, nor is it that they are so structurally dissimilar that the phrase could not easily be inserted. For example, article 21 states that "[n]o restrictions may be placed on the exercise of this right other than those imposed in conformity with the law and which are necessary in a democratic society" (listing the legitimating grounds), which is not unlike the wording of article 19, which says that the freedom of expression "may... be subject to certain restrictions, but these shall only be such as are provided by law and are necessary" (listing very similar legitimating grounds). Likewise, while the word "democracy" or "democratic" is found liberally in the preamble and the different articles in the American Convention, it is not present in article 13 on freedom of expression, whilst it is prominent, especially in articles 6–11, in the European Convention.

The HRC and the IACtHR have dealt with this ambiguity in different ways, the IACtHR more openly then the HRC, but both have managed to read-in the qualifier "in a democratic society" into their jurisprudence. Given the fact of its Cold War creation, the HRC has had a more difficult time of including this qualifier – it could well have been "necessary in a Marxist/theocratic/Confucian society" – and has only managed to do so more recently. While the absence of the now all-too-familiar phrase maybe difficult to explain, its later inclusion in the jurisprudence might be a bit easier as the substantive concept of rights in a democracy offers an anchor in an interpretative quandary. The significance in this will be discussed later in the article, but suffice it to say that this word and the guide that it represents has managed to find its way differently in the jurisprudence of all of the courts.

The texts of the articles themselves show a recurring structure for, although they are different lengths, they nevertheless follow a specific pattern by first outlining the components of the right (to hold opinions and to receive and impart ideas)[12] which is followed by a list of basis for restrictions (legitimating grounds) which provide the limit of the right, which are, chief among them, the rights and reputation of others and the interests of public order and public morality.

III. The Scope

The scope of Freedom of Expression in all three courts seems remarkably similar covering most forms of what can be considered speech or expression. For instance, the IACtHR has defined the scope of article 13 thus:

> Article 13 indicates that freedom of thought and expression "includes freedom to seek, receive, and impart information and ideas of all kinds ..." This language establishes that those to whom the Convention applies not only have the right and freedom to express their own thoughts but also the right and freedom to seek, receive and impart information and ideas of all kinds ... It requires, on the one hand, that no one be arbitrarily limited or impeded in expressing his own thoughts. In that sense, it is a right that belongs to each individual. Its second aspect ... implies a collective right to receive any information whatsoever and to have access to the thoughts expressed by others.

> ... It also includes and cannot be separated from the right *to use whatever medium is deemed appropriate* to impart ideas and to have them reach as wide an audience as possible ... This means that restrictions that are imposed on dissemination represent, in equal measure, a direct limitation on the right to express oneself freely.[13] (Emphasis added)

Correspondingly, the Human Rights Committee in its Commentary to article 19[14] has the fallowing explanation regarding scope:

> Paragraph 2 requires State parties to guarantee the right to freedom of expression, including the right to seek, receive and impart information and ideas of all kinds regardless of frontiers. This right includes the expression and receipt of communications of every form of idea and opinion capable of transmission to others, subject to the provisions in article 19, paragraph 3, and article 20 ... The scope of paragraph 2 embraces even expression that may be regarded as deeply offensive, although such expression may be restricted in accordance with the provisions of article 19, paragraph 3 and article 20.
> Paragraph 2 protects all forms of expression and the means of their dissemination. (Footnotes omitted)[15]

The ECtHR likewise follows this broad inclusion of the notion of expression in its scope of protection, where article 10 protects the freedom to hold opinions as well as the right to impart information and ideas, subject to limitations found in para 2. This includes all forms of expression delivered through any medium which in the past has included "paintings, books, cartoons, films, video-recordings, statements in radio interviews, information pamphlets and the internet"[16] that

> ... is applicable not only to "information" or "ideas" that are favourably received or regarded as inoffensive or as a matter of indifference, but also those that offend, shock or disturb the State or any sector of the population. Such are the demands of that pluralism, tolerance and broadmindedness without which there is no "democratic" society.[17]

There is, however, a difference in scope that can prove quite significant when it comes to the protection of expression between the IACtHR and the other two courts, namely in the IACtHR's exclusion of the possibility of so-called prior restraint (an action where a state can limit an expression before it is transmitted). Due to the specific choice of the drafters of the American Convention, article 13 explicitly states that "[t]he exercise of the right provided for in the foregoing paragraph shall not be subject to prior censorship but shall be subject to subsequent imposition of liability," with the exception of "public entertainments [which] may be subject by law to prior censorship for the sole purpose of regulating access to them for the moral protection of childhood and adolescence".[18] The IACtHR has elaborated upon this *inter alia* in the case of *Palamara-Iribarne v Chille*[19] where the court had to review the seizure and destruction, followed by an imposition of a fine and a ban on future publication of a book by Chilean authorities written by a former Naval officer regarding the ethics of the intelligence services. The court said that:

> ... Not every breach of Article 13 of the Convention entails an outright denial of the right to freedom of expression, which occurs when government power is used to establish means to prevent the free flow of information, ideas, opinions or news. Examples of this type of violation are prior censorship, seizure or banning of publications and, in general, any measures that subject expression or dissemination of information to State control ...[20]

Moreover, the court said that the state had a positive obligation not only to "allow him to write his ideas and opinions" but to also "enabl[e] him to distribute his book by any appropriate means to make his ideas and opinions reach the maximum number of people and, in turn, allowing these people to receive this information".[21]

On the other hand, there is nothing in the wording of the convention or in the jurisprudence of the ECtHR regarding *a priori* prevention of media from publishing controversial content and it has specifically said in its jurisprudence[22] that "[f]or the avoidance of doubt ... Article 10 of the Convention does not in terms prohibit the imposition of prior restraints on publication, as such. This is evidenced not only by the words "conditions", "restrictions", "preventing" and "prevention" which appear in that provision, but also by the Court's [jurisprudence]". However, because of the inherent dangers of prior restraint, its usage calls "for the most careful scrutiny on the part of the court. This is especially so as far as the press is concerned, *for news is a perishable commodity* and to delay its publication, even for a short period, may well deprive it of all its value and interest".[23] Consequently, when the issue of prior restraint reaches the court it takes on a standard proportionality analysis albeit with a much more stringent "necessity" requirements within the test. For instance, when a prior restraint issue arose in the case of *Gawęda v Poland*[24] the ECtHR found Poland to be in violation of the European Convention regarding the impreciseness of its media law which allowed for the refusal of a registration of a periodical under the grounds that it was not compatible (as the Polish media law put it) "with the real state of affairs". The court found that the requirement of an interference being prescribed by law is that the measure that has been undertaken by the authorities is foreseeable. Therefore, a norm, in order for it to be regarded as "law" it must be "formulated with sufficient precision to enable the citizen to regulate his conduct: he must be able – if need be with appropriate advice – to foresee, to a degree that is reasonable in the circumstances, the consequences which a given action may entail". Moreover:

> The Court considers that, although Article 10 of the Convention does not in terms prohibit the imposition of prior restraints on publications ..., the relevant law must provide a clear indication of the circumstances when such restraints are permissible and, *a fortiori*, when the consequences of the restraint are to block publication of a periodical completely, as in the present case. This is so because of the potential threat that such prior restraints, by their very nature, pose to the freedom of expression guaranteed by Article 10.[25]

However, some judges, notably in the dissent camp though, also think that the exercise of prior restraint by a state would trigger an automatic violation of article 10 except for instances provided for in article 15 derogations. In the *Spycatcher* case, the dissenting judges have noted, quoting Justice Black from the US Supreme Court in the *Pentagon Papers*[26] case, that:

> the press must be left free to publish news, "whatever the source, without censorship, injunctions, or prior restraint": in a free and democratic society there can be no room, in time of peace, for restrictions of that kind, and particularly not if these are resorted to, as they were in the present case, for "governmental suppression of embarrassing information" or ideas ...[27]

While this view has remained in the minority[28] it is still a potent view. Nevertheless, the court has even quite recently[29] confirmed its stance on prior restraint as a possible measure under the convention, albeit with a heavy burden of proof as to the necessity of the measure that is to be provided by the state.[30]

The HRC has been quite ambiguous about the issue of prior restraint. In its comments it has noted that "a free, uncensored and unhindered press or other media is essential in any society to ensure freedom of opinion and expression and the enjoyment of other Covenant rights", and that "[t]he free communication of information and ideas about public and political issues between citizens, candidates and elected representatives is essential" which implies, consequently, that the "free press and other media [are] able to comment on public issues without censorship or restraint and to inform public opinion".[31] However, the HRC has not had the opportunity to rule on this issue and, therefore, it is unclear whether prior restraint would be considered as outright breach of the convention (like in the IACtHR) or whether the HRC would use its standard proportionality analysis (like the ECtHR).

In addition, with reference to the scope of the conventions, it is worth noting that under all three conventions, as they are interpreted, the member states have both negative (not to interfere unduly with the right) and positive obligations. In the IACtHR, two cases against Venezuela highlight the extended scope of freedom of expression protection by the court for it found that Venezuela has violated the convention regarding article 13 when it: (1) made certain statements that "amount to a form of interference with or pressure impairing the rights of those who intend to contribute to public deliberation";[32] and (2) did not take sufficient steps to investigate threats against, and protect from attack, journalists critical of the government, regardless of the fact that those threats and attacks originated from private persons.[33]

In a similar case in the ECtHR regarding the member states' positive obligation to protect journalists and media from attacks by private persons, the court has said that "Genuine, effective exercise of freedom [of expression] does not depend merely on the State's duty not to interfere, but may require positive measures of protection, even in the sphere of relations between individuals". It also set out parameters regarding the determination of whether a positive obligation exists, specifically, that states have to take care that a "fair balance ... has to be struck between the general interest of the community and the interests of the individual, the search for which is inherent throughout the Convention". [34] The scope of this positive obligation varies, according to the court, and it will depend on the specific circumstances at hand, as well as "the difficulties involved in policing modern societies and the choices which must be made in terms of priorities and resources".[35] Moreover, the positive obligation must not be interpreted so as to present an extraordinary burden on states.[36]

The CHR, has not explicitly used, at least in its article 19 jurisprudence, the term "positive obligations" of member states, but it has however clearly stated in its Commentary on article 19[37] and in its Commentary on obligations of states (No 31)[38] that the "obligation to respect freedoms of opinion and expression ... also requires States parties to ensure that persons are protected from any acts by private persons or entities that would impair the enjoyment of the freedoms of opinion and expression to the extent that these Covenant rights are amenable to application between private persons or entities".[39] The case of *Gauthier v Canada*[40] could well be said to have been was settled on the grounds of the positive obligation of to ensure that a system of access to its parliamentary deliberations by journalists be "specific, fair and reasonable, and [its] application should be transparent"[41] even though it was operated under the control of a private entity, in this case the Canadian Press Gallery Association.

IV. Tests

There seems to be, at least on the surface, an almost complete overlap between the three jurisdictions when it comes to the tests they use to determine whether there has been a violation of the freedom of expression, i.e. the proportionality test. The ECtHR, given its early start in dealing with cases, is the natural leader in its elaboration and it would seem that, at least when it comes to the IACtHR, it is also a source of inspiration since the European Court is cited very prominently and given high regard in the IACtHR's earlier opinions. For instance, whole passages of ECtHR judgments were quoted in the IACtHR's first case dealing with freedom of expression, the *Advisory Opinion on Compulsory Membership*[42] as well as in the *Last Temptation of Christ* case,[43] while later any references to the ECtHR are put into footnotes.

The proportionality test has its origins in German constitutional law, which later spread to the ECtHR and the European Court of Justice (as well as other national courts) and from there to other international courts.[44] The test is composed of four parts, each structured around a seemingly commonsensical question: whether there was an interference; whether it was prescribed by law; whether it pursued a legitimate aim; and whether it was necessary/ proportionate to achieve that aim (or necessary in a democratic society). In some instances, there are prior issues that the courts need to address before progressing through the test, most notably the issue of whether the interest at stake or the nature of the complaint falls within the scope of the convention right in question.

A. Was there an interference?

The first prong of the test is often omitted since in most cases it is clear that there was an interference with the right. The IACtHR often, in this part of the test, has a discussion about the nature of the freedom of expression by discussing the individual and social dimension of opinion and speech as well as the negative and positive duties of the state to provide fertile ground for expression, and not to discriminate and create a plural media environment.[45] Similarly, the ECtHR starts with an affirmation of general principles that govern the law of a specific topic, including freedom of expression, which is then followed, if necessary, by a discussion of whether there was an interference with the right. The HRC, on the other hand, has the habit of only mentioning those prongs of the test that seem pertinent to the decision and can sometimes jump directly to the last prong of the test, the balancing phase.

B. Prescribed by law?

The second prong of the test looks at whether the action or the public authority that interfered with the right has a legal basis to do so. All of the courts in question have certain substantive requirements regarding the law's quality or origin that can generally fall under the understanding of rule of law requirements: the public character and availability of the norm in question, its coherence and its predictability. For instance, HRC's Commentary states, in relation to the "prescribed by law" requirement, that, given the fact that restrictions on the freedom of expression constitute a serious curtailment of rights, those restrictions cannot be "enshrined in traditional, religious or other such customary law".[46] Moreover, for a norm to be characterised as "law" under the ICCPR, it has to be "formulated with sufficient precision to enable an individual to regulate his or her conduct accordingly and it must be made accessible to the public". [47] Furthermore, the norms cannot give unfettered discretion to the authorities restricting the freedom of expression and they must "provide sufficient guidance to those charged with their execution to enable them to ascertain what sorts of expression are properly restricted and what sorts are not". [48]

The IACtHR has similar substantive requirements of the law prescribing the interference of the right in question. It has said, for instance, that the restrictions on the freedom of expression "must have been established by law" and that they are not "at the discretion of public authorities", that they are enacted "for reasons of general interest". Moreover, no legal norm can be accepted as a "synonym" of the word "law" even though they are set in a provision of a general nature.[49] Laws in this sense must be "adopted for the general welfare ... a concept that must be interpreted as an integral element of public order (*ordre public*) in democratic States ..."[50] Moreover, it has also said in relation to the imposition of criminal punishment that any limitations must be "formally and materially provided by law" and that they meet the strict requirements of the principle of *nullum crimen nulla poena sine lege previa*. Therefore, "they must be formulated previously, in an express, accurate, and restrictive manner". [51]

The ECtHR settled early on the issue of the substantive requirements that the term "law" is supposed to have. In the *Sunday Times* case it said that "the word 'law' in the expression 'prescribed by law' covers not only statute but also unwritten law",[52] noting that the intention of parties to the ECHR was not to exclude the common law from the term law. In the next paragraph it set out two criteria that flow from the expression "prescribed by law", and that is that "[f]irstly, the law must be adequately accessible, ... [and] [s]econdly, a norm cannot be regarded as a 'law' unless it is formulated with sufficient precision to enable the citizen to regulate his conduct: he must be able – if need be with appropriate advice – to foresee, to a degree that is reasonable in the circumstances, the consequences which a given action may entail".[53]

This paragraph is in essence outlines the ECtHR's three-part test assessing whether an interference was prescribed by law, in short (1) whether the interference has some legal basis either in statute or case-law, (2) whether it was accessible to the public, and (3) whether it was foreseeable even if the individual may need professional assistance to understand the law's requirements.[54] When it comes to the extent of the law's ambiguity, the court noted that laws and regulations need be "laid down with reasonable precision in accessible legal rules that sufficiently indicated the scope and manner of exercise of the discretion conferred on the relevant authorities".[55]

Some of the particularities of the three systems can be seen by contrasting these three substantive notions of the "prescribed by law" standard. For example, the HRC has ruled out "traditional, religious or any such customary law"[56] for reasons that have to do with states that use religious or local customary law as "law" in the sense that it is allowed or mandated for use in private or public relations (like customary or Sharia law in certain parts in Africa and Asia). However, the HRC certainly does not have in mind Anglo/Saxon common law as customary law even though the later can be a source of the former.[57] On the other hand, when the ECtHR speaks about unwritten law, it mentions the British/Anglo Saxon common law system in particular and it is far from its mind to consider that this type of law would be imprecise or unaccessible. Regardless of the idiosyncrasies of the three systems, they nonetheless have a similar notion of what attributes make something fall under the category of law and it is firmly based in the liberal rule of law tradition.

C. A legitimate aim?

The third prong of the test is quite similar across the three courts, the legitimating aim, which has slight variations depending on the wording of the articles in question, discussed above. There is also a difference in the strictness of the approach towards the matching of the state's action to the legitimating ground. The ECtHR, for example, has a very relaxed attitude towards the states' claims of following a legitimate aim and for not requiring a very strict connection between the state action and the legitimate aim pursued.

The issue is a bit more ambiguous when it comes to the IACtHR, however. The IACtHR had to struggle with an argument presented by Venezuela in the *Uson Ramirez* case,[58] which revolved around the applicant's conviction for the crime of slander of the Venezuelan Armed Forces. The issue of relevance here is the question as to whether the honour and reputation of the Armed Forces as an institution can be a legitimate aim under the Convention. The IACtHR had to distinguish two issues: whether institutions could be said to be entitled to have the right to honour and reputation under the Convention; and whether the reputation and honour of an institution could be a legitimating ground for which the Convention wording was ambiguous.[59] In drew inspiration from the ECtHR, which has recognised companies as entities that have reputation interests, and consequently decided to accept that the meaning of the phrase "the reputation of others" also includes institutions like the Venezuelan Armed Forces.[60]

The HRC on the other hand has strict guidelines regarding the stated connection between the restriction and the legitimate aim pursued. For instance, in its Article 19 Commentary it has stated that if a legitimating ground is invoked, the state "must demonstrate in specific and individualized fashion the precise nature of the threat, and the necessity and proportionality of the specific action taken, in particular by establishing a direct and immediate connection between the expression and the threat".[61] The final assessment is left to the discretion of the HRC.

D. Necessity – proportionality in the narrow sense

The fourth prong of the test, necessity, is arguably the most important part of the proportionality test and is where the most of the cases are decided. Because this part of the test is so frequently used, the ECtHR has even set up a test within a test, specified in the *Silver*[62] case, saying that

> On a number of occasions, the Court has stated its understanding of the phrase "necessary in a democratic society", the nature of its functions in the examination of issues turning on that phrase and the manner in which it will perform those functions. It suffices here to summarise certain principles:
>
> (a) the adjective "necessary" is not synonymous with "indispensable", neither has it the flexibility of such expressions as "admissible", "ordinary", "useful", "reasonable" or "desirable" ...;
> (b) the Contracting States enjoy a certain but not unlimited margin of appreciation in the matter of the imposition of restrictions, but it is for the Court to give the final ruling on whether they are compatible with the Convention ...;

(c) the phrase "necessary in a democratic society" means that, to be compatible with the Convention, the interference must, inter alia, correspond to a "pressing social need" and be "proportionate to the legitimate aim pursued" ...;
(d) those paragraphs of Articles of the Convention which provide for an exception to a right guaranteed are to be narrowly interpreted ...[63]

In general, what is required by this test is for a state to show that for a measure to be necessary in a democratic society it has to be undertaken as a "response to a pressing social need, and that the interference with the rights protected is no greater than is necessary to address that pressing social need".[64] Moreover, as it is related to the ECtHR, it is where the crucial margin of appreciation doctrine comes into play and where some of the uncertainty as to specific case-by-case application is the strongest.[65] Nevertheless, it seems that some of the uncertainty is alleviated when the freedom of expression is put in the context of who writes what, for what audience and, in case of post facto sanctions, the nature of the punishment. For instance, the ECtHR has said that criticism of the government enjoys greater leeway especially if it is uttered by politicians or journalists, and that a heavy penalty such as a prison sentence is greatly discouraged.[66]

The IACtHR has a very similar approach when it comes to the balancing aspect of the proportionality test. However, first let us look at how the standard of necessary in *a democratic society* came to be present at the court. In its first opinion dealing with Article 13 and elaborating on the test that it needed to apply the IACtHR said that:

> The Court must also take account of the Preamble of the Convention in which the signatory states reaffirm "their intention to consolidate in this hemisphere, within the framework of democratic institutions, a system of personal liberty and social justice based on respect for the essential rights of man". These articles define the context within which the restrictions permitted under Article 13(2) must be interpreted. It follows from the repeated reference to "democratic institutions", "representative democracy" and "democratic society" that the question whether a restriction on freedom of expression imposed by a state is "necessary to ensure" one of the objectives listed in subparagraphs (a) or (b) must be judged by reference to the legitimate needs of democratic societies and institutions.

The IACtHR then went on to compare the wording of the ACHR freedom of expression article 13 with that of the ECHR's article 10, noting the lack of the phrase "necessary in a democratic society" in article 13. However, it deflected this absence by invoking article 29 of the ACHR which prohibits the interpretation of the ACHR which would preclude "other rights and guarantees ... derived from representative democracy as a form of government".[67] Moreover, "[t]he just demands of democracy must consequently guide the interpretation of the Convention and, in particular, the interpretation of those provisions that bear a critical relationship to the preservation and functioning of democratic institutions".[68]

When it comes to necessity, the IACtHR has adopted a similar wording to that used by the ECtHR using its jurisprudence as an inspiration.[69] While it has not elaborated a separate test within a test as the ECtHR has, it has used means-ends wording in its reasoning. For instance, when defining necessity it said that the legality of a restriction depends "upon [the] showing that the restrictions are required by a compelling governmental interest"[70] and that the least restrictive measure has been selected from those available. Therefore, "it is not enough to demonstrate ... that a law performs a useful or desirable purpose; to be compatible with the Convention, the restrictions must be justified by reference to governmental objectives which, because of their importance, clearly outweigh the social need for the full enjoyment of the right Article 13 guarantees".[71] Moreover, the restriction itself "must be proportionate and closely tailored to the accomplishment of the legitimate governmental objective necessitating it".[72]

Despite the fact that the IACtHR was inspired by the ECtHR in its proportionality test, it has not, however, adopted the controversial doctrine of the margin of appreciation and, to my knowledge, has remained ambivalent to it. Some claim[73] that the IACtHR is on the path to developing a doctrine of a margin of appreciation, or something similar, since the states in the American system are becoming stable democracies and the cases coming to the IACtHR are becoming more complicated and far less clear-cut issues of violation of rights and, consequently, the IACtHR will be forced to develop, if it has not already developed, a deference doctrine. Because this may turn out to be a crucial question in assessing the dangers of fragmentation between the ECtHR and the rest, it is important to give some overview of the margin of appreciation doctrine.

The margin of appreciation doctrine has been around as part of the ECtHR for the past four decades. It was first used by the former European Commission on Human Rights and was used by the court in the *Ireland v UK* judgment[74] for the first time.[75] The doctrine has its origins in French administrative law[76] and as such it is a deference doctrine of the court given to other branches of government, most notably the administration but also the regulators in deciding the scope and means of implementing legislation on the grounds that those administrators or regulators are better placed to make a judgment within their discretion on the balance of facts. In this instance, a reviewing court would then scrutinise whether the body has stayed within the margins of its discretion and whether it has taken the proper considerations into account when making its decision. In this sense, one could say that a deference doctrine is part of the understanding of what a normal rights reviewing court is supposed to do, either through a standard of review of reasonableness or something similar.

Throughout its use at the ECtHR, however, it has developed into two concepts:[77] substantive, which "address[es] the relationship between individual freedoms and collective goals"[78] and is originally imported from domestic law, and the structural which "is to address the limits or intensity of the review of the [ECtHR] in view of its status as an international tribunal".[79] The two concepts and the ECtHR's lack of a clear distinction of which concept is used when and under which circumstances creates an unpredictable jurisprudence, to the extent that some commentators have called the margin of appreciation doctrine "slippery and elusive as an eel [and that a]gain and again the Court now appears to use the margin of appreciation as a substitute for coherent legal analysis of the issues at stake".[80] Judge De Meyer said that "it is high time for the Court to banish that [margin of appreciation] concept from its reasoning"[81] back in 1997, albeit citing not only its circumlocution, which was evident at the time, but also the smell of relativism that it brought with it. Recently, it has been said that the margin possess "a variable geometry"[82] that it is a "threat to the rule of law"[83] and that is a doctrine that has no more and no less than seven factors to determine its width.[84] The shape of the doctrine is widely discussed both in ECtHR judgments[85] as well as in academic literature[86] with no definite conclusion on its shape and scope, or even its utility.

When it comes to the IACtHR there is, to some extent, reference to margin in at least two cases of the IACtHR, most notably the *Ricardo Canese* case,[87] and even more importantly following discussion of the proportionality test, which in the ECtHR is one of the prongs of the necessity test. The court says:

> The Court has indicated that the "necessity" and, hence, the legality of restrictions imposed on freedom of expression under Article 13(2) of the American Convention, depend upon showing

> that the restrictions are required by a compelling public interest ... In other words, the restriction must be proportionate to the interest that justifies it and closely tailored to accomplishing this legitimate objective, interfering as little as possible with the effective exercise of the right to freedom of expression.
> Democratic control exercised by society through public opinion encourages the transparency of State activities and promotes the accountability of public officials in public administration, for which there should be a reduced margin for any restriction on political debates or on debates on matters of public interest. (Footnotes omitted) [88]

The IACtHR seems to argue here for a margin on a sliding scale depending on factors which are similar to Letsas' substantive notion, finding the proper balance between individual freedoms and collective goals. However, as of yet the IACtHR has not elaborated any further on what this margin, if it exists, is and what it entails. I may very well imply the introduction of a margin of appreciation doctrine, yet, given the fact that this case was decided in 2004, almost 10 years ago, and given that there has not been much development on that front regarding a discussion on any type of margin for states (something that is proving to be a crucial doctrine in the ECtHR), I hesitate to say that there is such a thing as a margin of appreciation-type doctrine at the IACtHR, at least not in the structural sense that Letsas has defined.[89] As I have argued earlier, some sort of deference doctrine is ingrained in rights review, simply because judicial review in most cases comes after other branches have decided on certain issues touching on the rights of individuals, which, in most instances, involve some sort of discretion in the creation or application of the rules – a margin if you will. Consequently a part of a reviewing court's task (any court, national or international), when it carries out a rights review, is to afford such deference. In that sense, not having a deference doctrine (whether it is called a reasonableness review, strict scrutiny or proportionality *stricto sensu*) would be the surprise, not *vice versa*. But whether that doctrine of deference takes the shape of a margin of appreciation doctrine in its structural sense as is currently in growing importance at the ECtHR, is far from clear and as of yet I am not convinced by Legg's argument of its existence in the IACtHR.

The HRC is a different story, however. It has not remained silent on the issue of the margin of appreciation and it has specifically rejected it. It has said as early as 1994[90] that a state's "scope of its freedom to ... [take a certain action] is not to be assessed by reference to a margin of appreciation, but by reference to the obligations it has undertaken"[91] under the Covenant (in this case the HRC was talking about economic regulation and obligations under article 27). Finland in that case specifically argued for the inclusion of the margin of appreciation doctrine in the HRC's deliberation process, citing the ECtHR as its example. In that sense, the HRC has rejected the margin of appreciation doctrine as practised by the ECtHR, a rejection which it has reiterated with the recent Commentary on Article 19 where it said that "the Committee recalls that the scope of this freedom [i.e. freedom of expression] is not to be assessed by reference to a 'margin of appreciation'". Given the discussion in the previous paragraph it is reasonable to assume that what the HRC means by its rejection of the margin of appreciation is that the obligations of states would be decided based on the meaning of the relevant article in question, which would include the type of deference that is normal under rights review – Letsas' substantive concept. In a sense, the rejection of the HRC is the rejection of the margin of appreciation as the deference given to states simply because they are states, while it might be open that they are the ones who have to conduct a first instance balancing and because they have to weigh individual rights against public interest.

When it comes to the proportionality test, the three jurisdictions have an astonishing overlap, not only in the formal features of the test (i.e. four prongs requiring answers to similar questions) but also in the substantive requirements within the test, at least concerning freedom of expression. There is, however, a significant difference between the ECtHR and the other two courts, and that is in the doctrine of the margin of appreciation. While the ECtHR is not only fully committed[92] to the doctrine, it also has two competing concepts of it, about which the two other courts are either ambivalent (IACtHR) or reject outright (HRC). When it comes to fragmentation, and given the rising importance of the margin of appreciation doctrine in the ECtHR, the lack or rejection of such a crucial doctrine for one court but not for the others may result in a wider discrepancy of outcomes. This, may not ultimately be the case, at least when it comes to journalists and the media since, even the ECtHR acknowledges the narrowness of the margin in these instances. However, taken as a whole, the margin of appreciation doctrine may be too important a piece to be left out of any considerations of fragmentation for it certainly may lead to some quite surprising and divergent outcomes especially given the doctrine's unpredictability[93] at the moment.

V. Justifications

When it comes to the justifications of the wider protection of the freedom of expression of journalists and media, especially regarding public officials, again the overlap is quite considerable. In order to understand the context of justification, of why journalists and the media and freedom of expression generally is given such a high regard, its connection to the notion of democratic society must be understood not just as a system of governing. In this sense, it is society that must be democratic not just government. The ECtHR, for instance, sees the characteristics of a democratic society to be "pluralism, tolerance and broadmindedness without which there is no 'democratic society'".[94] Democratic societies are, therefore, plural and, as such, must exhibit tolerance and broadmindedness "not only to 'information' or 'ideas' that are favourably received or regarded as inoffensive or as a matter of indifference, but also to those that offend, shock or disturb the State or any sector of the population".[95] Consequently, "[f]reedom of expression constitutes one of the essential foundations of such a society, one of the basic conditions for its progress and for the development of every man".[96]

In this last sentence we have another type of justification for having a wide ranging freedom of expression that runs parallel with, but can sometimes conflict with, a democratic society, and that is that the freedom of expression is one of the basic conditions for the personal development of every person. While the previous conception of rights sees their purpose in fostering the existence of a democratic society (rights as enablers of democracy, a political conception of rights), the second sees rights in a deontic light where human rights are owed to each individual because every human being is endowed with reason and moral agency.[97] It is in this sense that rights are a necessary condition of the development of every person because, as creatures of reason, we require a bubble of autonomy expressed and secured by rights. In this sense rights are pre-political; they exist even in a so-called state of nature. Most of the time the proponents of these two views agree on the outcome, but they can sometimes produce conflicting results.

The IACtHR has a similar line of justification regarding its article 13 jurisprudence. When deciding of the proportionality of a state action to the legitimate aim it said that:

> … it shall be reiterated that in the test of proportionality it should be taken into account that the expressions about the exercise of the functions of the State Institutions have a greater protection, in the sense that they can promote a democratic debate in society. That is the case because it is supposed that in a democratic society the state institutions or entities as such are exposed to public scrutiny and criticism, and their activities are inserted in the domain of public debate. This threshold is not based on the quality of the subject but on the public interest of the activities carried out. Hence larger tolerance should face the affirmations and considerations made by citizens when exercising their democratic right. Such are the demands for pluralism of a truly democratic society, requiring a more significant circulation of reports and opinions about matters of public interest.[98]

Moreover,

> Freedom of expression is a cornerstone upon which the very existence of a democratic society rests. It is indispensable for the formation of public opinion. It is also a *conditio sine qua non* for the development of political parties, trade unions, scientific and cultural societies and, in general, those who wish to influence the public. It represents, in short, the means that enable the community, when exercising its options, to be sufficiently informed. Consequently, it can be said that a society that is not well informed is not a society that is truly free.
> Within this context, journalism is the primary and principal manifestation of freedom of expression of thought. For that reason, because it is linked with freedom of expression, which is an inherent right of each individual, journalism cannot be equated to a profession that is merely granting a service to the public through the application of some knowledge or training acquired in a university or through those who are enrolled in a certain professional 'colegio'.[99]

Furthermore, the IACtHR took pains to highlight the identity of its approach of its concept of the freedom of expression and its ties to democracy with those taken by other international courts and bodies:

> Thus, the different regional systems for the protection of human rights and the universal system agree on the essential role played by freedom of expression in the consolidation and dynamics of a democratic society. Without effective freedom of expression, exercised in all its forms, democracy is enervated, pluralism and tolerance start to deteriorate, the mechanisms for control and complaint by the individual become ineffectual and, above all, a fertile ground is created for authoritarian systems to take root in society.[100]

Again, the mix of justifications is noticeable: on the one hand freedom of expression protects the democratic nature of a society, highlighting the freedom's political nature, but on the other hand it is an inherent right of each individual which exists regardless of whether it protects democracy or not. The outcomes in practice may be quite similar under both conceptions, nevertheless, the IACtHR, and the ECtHR, are not particularly concerned with possible contradictions that the different grounding of rights can deliver.

The HRC is not far behind the ECtHR and the IACtHR in the type of justifications offered for the freedom of expression. The opening paragraphs of General Comment No 34 attest to that thus:

> Freedom of opinion and freedom of expression are indispensable conditions for the full development of the person. They are essential for any society. They constitute the foundation stone for every free and democratic society. The two freedoms are closely related, with freedom of expression providing the vehicle for the exchange and development of opinions.

Freedom of expression is a necessary condition for the realisation of the principles of transparency and accountability that are, in turn, essential for the promotion and protection of human rights.[101]

It is interesting how the HRC layers its justification of article 19. It first starts with the two rights that come under article 19, freedom of opinion, which it deems non-derogable,[102] and freedom of expression, which is a qualified right due to the fact that it is "the vehicle for the exchange and development of opinions",[103] meaning that while a state cannot and should not stop a person from holding opinions, from reasoning (a hallmark of a human being as a thinking animal), their outward expression as well as their exchange can be limited since the voicing of some opinions is preferred to others. One may hate as many groups as one wishes, but the expression of that hatred (one's outward voicing of it), however, can very well be limited. While a state cannot and should not try to stop one from thinking, it can certainly limit what you say out loud. Furthermore, it sees both the freedom to hold opinions and the freedom of expression as "indispensable to the development of any person"[104] and that they "are essential for any society".[105] They are, however, "the foundation stone for every free and democratic society".[106] In a single paragraph the HRC seems to manage to ground the freedom of expression and the freedom to hold opinions in two doctrines, since they are essential for any society and therefore any single human being (how can a society exist if (a) humans cannot reason and therefore hold opinions about anything and everything, and (b) they cannot communicate). They are not bound to a single political ideal, they are wherever society exists,[107] but are at the same time the foundation stone of a free and democratic society. In order for a democratic society to exist, freedom of expression and, by extension, freedom of the press, must exist with article 19 presenting the maximum amount of limitation that a state can deploy and still be considered democratic.

VI. Conclusions

While reading through the judgments of the three courts, I cannot but be startled by their similarity. Yes, they are different in many ways, the length of the written opinion being one prominent example. Yet when one looks at them in their entirety, they have a remarkably similar structure. The opinions open with an exposition of the legally relevant facts or, in the situation of the IACtHR, with the facts that were presented during the hearing, and in writing and the assessment of their veracity. The facts can and often do include the judgments or decisions of local authorities, statements from public officials which are relevant and, in the case of the IACtHR, witness testimonies. The courts then continue by summarising the arguments that the states and the applicants make, and finish with their own assessment. Ultimately, the assessment of the arguments in all three courts is carried out through the steps of the proportionality analysis which is more or less formalised and formulaic (depending on the court in question; as I mentioned earlier, the HRC may skip steps).

It is not only that the structure of the written opinions follows a similar pattern, but the substance in those parts follows a similar wording as well. Moreover, the identity of justifications or the understanding of what rights are for, and what their purpose is, offers a further stabilising element which allows for an exchange of influence between the courts. To put it in another way, if there were not a shared understanding regarding the substantive requirements of the rights and their purpose, there would hardly be any reason for looking at and being influenced by the jurisprudence of the other courts. It is only if there is an understanding that the courts themselves are involved in a similar enterprise, that they share similar values and purposes, that they will find the other courts' reasoning persuasive or authoritative.

There are at least two great outliers in the system when it comes to the protection of freedom of expression and in relation to journalism, and those are the issue of prior restraint and the margin of appreciation doctrine. While the way that prior restraint is formulated in the IACtHR gives a high level of predictability (prior restraint is excluded except for the protection of minors), the other two systems put acts of prior restraint through their normal channels of analysis, albeit with an increasing threshold of proportionality for the state to pass. While in practice this might result in a significant conversion of outcomes, i.e. most instances of prior restraint would be found to be a violation, nevertheless, the fact remains that if the *Spycatcher* case[108] had been argued before the IACtHR, it would have found a violation of article 13 for the whole duration of the publication ban and not just after the content of the book became public outside the UK.[109]

A bigger outlier, however, is the doctrine of the margin of appreciation, as this doctrine plays an increasingly crucial role in the ECtHR reasoning at the same time as it has been rejected by the HRC and the IACtHR has been mostly silent on the matter. It might be the case, at least for the IACtHR, that the fact that that court is faced with mostly clear-cut cases of rights violations that it has not yet had the need to develop any deference doctrine such as the margin of appreciation. On the other hand, the HRC's rejection of the doctrine can be explained by the environment in which it operates and the extreme inter-regional diversity that is very different from the relative intra-regional homogeneity[110] of the other two systems. Moreover, the charges of relativism that have been levied against the doctrine may have influenced the HRC's rejection of it. In such an environment the HRC may be more concerned with having a common standard for all rather than allowing for a margin of appreciation based on local conceptions of morals and national security, for example. Regardless of the reasons, and to a large extent due to the unpredictability of the doctrine itself, there might very well be a difficulty in synchronising the jurisprudence between the courts, especially if the ECtHR continues to relay on it to do the "heavy lifting" in controversial issues. Let us not forget that part of the doctrine requires the ECtHR to follow national trends when interpreting the convention and determining the extent of the margin. This doctrinal divergence can to a large extent frustrate the trend of the courts looking at each other's jurisprudence for at least two reasons: (a) the practical problem of following the national trends of the Council of Europe members in order to anticipate the development of the ECtHR's margin of appreciation in specific fields, and (b) the wider conceptual issue of why pegging the development of rights to the national trends of the members of the Council of Europe, given the difference in the needs of systems that the other courts operate. If the ECtHR keeps basing its rights protection on the national trends of Council of Europe members, then it is moving further and further away from the concept of "normative equivalence" for it will see the rights not as rights stemming from the common understanding found in the Universal Declaration but in the common understanding of European states. To the extent that the two differ, the ECtHR may be signalling to the other courts that it may wish to disassociate itself from the Universal Declaration and therefore with the rest of the world.

Regardless of this trend, one conclusion cannot be avoided, and that is that given the structure through which the reasoning process is carried out, coupled with the high level of shared understanding of the concept of rights and their place in a democratic society, it is not difficult to imagine that most of the cases coming before these courts would be settled in a similar manner. It seems that the shared values and identity of these courts makes them highly motivated to look at what their peer institutions are doing, and following their insights. There is much more that these courts share than what divides them and that is what will, ultimately, keep them in roughly the same normative box with very little competition between each other, at least as far as when the freedom of expression and journalisms is concerned.

Acknowledgements

This article was presented as part of a workshop funded by the MultiRights project. I wish to thank the participants to the workshop "Fragmentation of International Human Rights – Beyond the Conflict of Laws" held at the Central European University in Budapest – Lucas Lixinski, Svetlana Tylkina, Orsolya Salát, Kristin Henrard, Andreas Føllesdal, and Renata Uitz for helpful and lively discussion. I would also like to thank the Board and the reviewers of this journal for their comments; they were very helpful. And last, but not least, I wish to thank Natasha Telson for her Herculean efforts in facilitating the coordination of the whole issue.

Notes

1. M Koskenniemi, *Report on Fragmentation of International Law: Difficulties Arising from the Diversification and Expansion of International Law* (International Law Commission, Geneva, UN Doc A/CN.4/L.682, 2006).
2. T Broude and Y Shany (eds), *Multi-Sourced Equivalent Norms in International Law* (Studies in International Law, Hart Publishing, Oxford, Portland, OR, 2013).
3. For the sake of expedience in the continuation of the article, all of these institutions will be called courts.
4. General Assembly resolution 217 A (III), 10 December 1948.
5. P van Dijk, GJH van Hoof, A van Rijn and L Zwaak (eds), *Theory and Practice of the European Convention on Human Rights* (Intersentia, Antwerp, 2006); R Hanski, M Scheinin, UNHR Committee and Åalfm Rättigheter, *Leading Cases of the Human Rights Committee* (Institut for Human Rights, Åbo Akademi University, 2007); L Burgorgue-Larsen, A Úbeda de Torres and R Greenstein, *The Inter-American Court of Human Rights: Case-Law and Commentary* (Oxford UP, Oxford, New York, 2011); and J Casadevali, E Myjer, M O'Boyle and A Austin (2012). *Freedom of Expression: Essays in Honour of Nicolas Bratza, President of the European Court of Human Rights* (Wolf Legal Publishers, Oisterwijk, 2012); AR Mowbray, *Cases and Materials on the European Convention on Human Rights* (Oxford UP, Oxford, 2007) and; AR Mowbray, *Cases, Materials, and Commentary on the European Convention on Human Rights* (Oxford UP, Oxford, 2012).
6. " … Considering that the aim of the Council of Europe is the achievement of greater unity between its members and that one of the methods by which that aim is to be pursued is the maintenance and further realisation of human rights and fundamental freedoms;Reaffirming their profound belief in those fundamental freedoms which are the foundation of justice and peace in the world and are best maintained on the one hand by an effective political democracy and on the other by a common understanding and observance of the human rights upon which they depend; Being resolved, as the governments of European countries which are like-minded and have a common heritage of political traditions, ideals, freedom and the rule of law, to take the first steps for the collective enforcement of certain of the rights stated in the Universal Declaration …"
7. "*Reaffirming* their intention to consolidate in this hemisphere, within the framework of democratic institutions, a system of personal liberty and social justice based on respect for the essential rights of man …"
8. "Considering that, in accordance with the principles proclaimed in the Charter of the United Nations, recognition of the inherent dignity and of the equal and inalienable rights of all members of the human family is the foundation of freedom, justice and peace in the world, …Considering the obligation of States under the Charter of the United Nations to promote universal respect for, and observance of, human rights and freedoms,
9. For the European Convention: " … Considering the Universal Declaration of Human Rights proclaimed by the General Assembly of the United Nations on 10th December 1948;Considering that this Declaration aims at securing the universal and effective recognition and observance of the

Rights therein declared ..." For the Covenant: " ... Recognizing that, in accordance with the Universal Declaration of Human Rights, the ideal of free human beings enjoying civil and political freedom and freedom from fear and want can only be achieved if conditions are created whereby everyone may enjoy his civil and political rights, as well as his economic, social and cultural rights ..." For the American Convention: " ... *Considering* that these principles have been set forth in the Charter of the Organization of American States, in the American Declaration of the Rights and Duties of Man, and in the Universal Declaration of Human Rights, and that they have been reaffirmed and refined in other international instruments, worldwide as well as regional in scope; *Reiterating* that, in accordance with the Universal Declaration of Human Rights, the ideal of free men enjoying freedom from fear and want can be achieved only if conditions are created whereby everyone may enjoy his economic, social, and cultural rights, as well as his civil and political rights; and ..."

10. Universal Declaration of Human Rights, General Assembly Resolution 217 A (III), 10 December 1948.
11. For the European Convention: " ... Reaffirming their profound belief in those fundamental freedoms which are the foundation of justice and peace in the world and are best maintained on the one hand by an effective political democracy and on the other by a common understanding and observance of the human rights upon which they depend ...
12. For the European Convention: "1. Everyone has the right to freedom of expression. This right shall include freedom to hold opinions and to receive and impart information and ideas without interference by public authority and regardless of frontiers"; for the Covenant: "Everyone shall have the right to hold opinions without interference. 2. Everyone shall have the right to freedom of expression; this right shall include freedom to seek, receive and impart information and ideas of all kinds, regardless of frontiers, either orally, in writing or in print, in the form of art, or through any other media of his choice"; and, for the American Convention: "1. Everyone has the right to freedom of thought and expression. This right includes freedom to seek, receive, and impart information and ideas of all kinds, regardless of frontiers, either orally, in writing, in print, in the form of art, or through any other medium of one's choice".
13. *Compulsory Membership in an Association Prescribed by Law for the Practice of Journalism (Arts 13 and 29 American Convention on Human Rights)*, Advisory Opinion OC-5/85, IACtHR, 13 November 1985, para s 30–31.
14. *General Comment No 34, Art 19, Freedoms of Opinion and Expression*, United Nations Human Rights Committee, 102nd Session, UN Doc CCPR/C/GC/34, 12 September 2011.
15. *General Comment No 34, Article 19, Freedoms of Opinion and Expression*, United Nations Human Rights Committee, 102nd Session, UN Doc CCPR/C/GC/34, 12 September 2011, at paras 11–12.
16. C Ovey, RCA White and FG Jacobs, *The European Convention on Human Rights* (Oxford UP, Oxford, 2010), at 426.
17. *Handyside v United Kingdom* (Application No 5493/72), Section judgment, ECtHR, 7 December 1976, at para 48.
18. Article 13, paras 2 and 4, American Convention on Human Rights.
19. *Case of Palamara-Iribarne v Chille (Merits, Reparations, and Costs)*, Judgment, IACtHR, 22 November 2005.
20. *Case of Palamara-Iribarne v Chille, (Merits, Reparations, and Costs)*, at para 68.
21. *Case of Palamara-Iribarne v Chille, (Merits, Reparations, and Costs)*, at para 71.
22. *Observer & Guardian v UK* (Application No 13585/88), Plenary session, ECtHR, 26 November 1991 (hereafter the *Spycatcher* case).
23. C Ovey, RCA White and FG Jacobs, *The European Convention on Human Rights* (Oxford UP, Oxford, 2010), at 69–70, para 60 (emphasis added).
24. *Gaweda v Poland* (Application No 26229/95), Section Judgment, ECtHR, 14 March 2002, but see also C Ovey, RCA White and FG Jacobs, *The European Convention on Human Rights* (Oxford UP, Oxford, 2010), at 61–63.
25. *Gaweda v Poland* (Application No 26229/95), Section Judgment, ECtHR, 14 March 2002, at paras 59–60.
26. *New York Times v United States* (1971) 403 US 713.

27. *Partially Dissenting Opinion by Judge de Meyer (Concerning Prior Restraint) joined by Judges Pettiti, Russo, Foighel and Bigi, Observer and Guardian v UK (Application No 13585/88)*, Plenary Session, ECtHR, 26 November 1991.
28. See the dissenting opinions in *Open Door & Dublin Well Woman v Ireland (Application No 14234/88; 14235/88)*, ECtHR, 29 October 1992.
29. *Yildirim v Turkey* (*Application No 3111/10*), ECHR, 18 December 2012.
30. "The Court reiterates that Article 10 does not prohibit prior restraints on publication as such. This is borne out not only by the words 'conditions', 'restrictions', 'preventing' and 'prevention' which appear in that provision, but also by the Court's judgment[s] ... On the other hand, the dangers inherent in prior restraints are such that they call for the most careful scrutiny on the part of the Court. This is especially so as far as the press is concerned, for news is a perishable commodity and to delay its publication, even for a short period, may well deprive it of all its value and interest. This danger also applies to publications other than periodicals that deal with a topical issue." *Yildirim v Turkey* (*Application No 3111/10*), ECHR, 18 December 2012, at para 47.
31. *General Comment No 34, Article 19, Freedoms of Opinion and Expression*, United Nations Human Rights Committee, 102nd Session, UN Doc CCPR/C/GC/34, 12 September 2011, at para 13.
32. *Case of Perozo v Venezuela (Preliminary Objections, Merits, Reparations, and Costs)*, Judgment IACtHR, 28 January 2009, at para 151.
33. *Case of Perozo v Venezuela (Preliminary Objections, Merits, Reparations, and Costs)*, Judgment IACtHR, 28 January 2009, at paras 151–61.
34. *Özgür Gündem v Turkey* (*Application No 23144/93*), ECtHR, 16 March 2000, at para 43.
35. *Özgür Gündem v Turkey* (*Application No 23144/93*), ECtHR, 16 March 2000.
36. *Özgür Gündem v Turkey* (*Application No 23144/93*), ECtHR, 16 March 2000.
37. *General Comment No 34, Article 19, Freedoms of Opinion and Expression*, United Nations Human Rights Committee, 102nd Session, UN Doc CCPR/C/GC/34, 12 September 2011, at para 7.
38. The Committee's General Comment No 31 (2004) on the nature of the general legal obligation imposed on States parties to the Covenant, *Official Records of the General Assembly, Fifty-ninth Session, Supplement No 40*, vol I (A/59/40 (Vol I)), annex III.
39. *General Comment No 34, Article 19, Freedoms of Opinion and Expression*, United Nations Human Rights Committee, 102nd Session, UN Doc CCPR/C/GC/34, 12 September 2011, at para 7.
40. *Gauthier v Canada, Communication No 633/1995*, UN Doc CCPR/C/65/D/633/1995 (5 May 1999).
41. *Gauthier v Canada, Communication No 633/1995*, UN Doc CCPR/C/65/D/633/1995 (5 May 1999), at para 13.6.
42. *Compulsory Membership in an Association Prescribed by Law for the Practice of Journalism (Arts. 13 and 29 American Convention on Human Rights)*, Advisory Opinion OC-5/85, IACtHR, 13 November 1985, paras 42–51.
43. *Case of "The Last Temptation of Christ" (Olmedo-Bustos et al.) v Chile (Merits, Reparations and Costs)*, Judgment, IACtHR, 5 February 2001.
44. AS Sweet and J Mathews, "Proportionality balancing and Global Constitutionalism" (2008) 47 *Columbia J of Transnational Law* 73–165, at 97–104.
45. *See cases Case of Perozo et al. v Venezuela (Preliminary Objections, Merits, Reparations, and Costs)*, Judgment, IACtHR, 28 January 2009 and *Case of Ríos et al. v Venezuela (Preliminary Objections, Merits, Reparations, and Costs)*, Judgment, IACtHR, 28 January 2009.
46. *General Comment No 34, Article 19, Freedoms of Opinion and Expression*, United Nations Human Rights Committee, 102nd Session, UN Doc CCPR/C/GC/34, 12 September 2011, at para 24.
47. *General Comment No 34, Article 19, Freedoms of Opinion and Expression*, United Nations Human Rights Committee, 102nd Session, UN Doc CCPR/C/GC/34, 12 September 2011, at para 26.
48. *General Comment No 34, Article 19, Freedoms of Opinion and Expression*, United Nations Human Rights Committee, 102nd Session, UN Doc CCPR/C/GC/34, 12 September 2011, at paras 24–26.
49. *Case of Claude-Reyes et al v Chile (Merits, Reparations and Costs)*, Judgment, IACtHR, 19 September 2006, at para 89.
50. *Case of Claude-Reyes et al v Chile (Merits, Reparations and Costs)*, Judgment, IACtHR, 19 September 2006, footnotes omitted.
51. *Case of Kimel v Argentina (Merits, Reparations and Costs)*, Judgment, IACtHR, 2 May 2008.
52. *Sunday Times v UK*, A.30 (1979) 2 EHRR 245, at para 47.

53. *Sunday Times v UK*, A.30 (1979) 2 EHRR 245, at para 49.
54. C Ovey, RCA White and FG Jacobs, *The European Convention on Human Rights* (Oxford UP, Oxford, 2010), at 312–15.
55. *Malone v United Kingdom (Application No 8691/79)*, Section judgment, ECtHR, 2 August 1984; see also C Ovey, RCA White and FG Jacobs, *The European Convention on Human Rights* (Oxford UP, Oxford, 2010), at 313–14.
56. *General Comment No 34, Article 19, Freedoms of Opinion and Expression*, United Nations Human Rights Committee, 102nd Session, UN Doc CCPR/C/GC/34, 12 September 2011, at para 24.
57. G Slapper and D Kelly, *The English Legal System, 2012–2013* (Routledge, London, 2012).
58. *Case of Usón Ramírez v Venezuela (Preliminary Objections, Merits, Reparations, and Costs)* Judgment, IACtHR, 20 November 2009.
59. *Case of Usón Ramírez v Venezuela (Preliminary Objections, Merits, Reparations, and Costs)* Judgment, IACtHR, 20 November 2009, at para 63; the IACtHR did not question the fact that only individuals are the beneficiaries of the rights under the Convention and, therefore, institutions do not have the right to honour as individuals do.
60. *Case of Usón Ramírez v Venezuela (Preliminary Objections, Merits, Reparations, and Costs)* Judgment, IACtHR, 20 November 2009, at para 65.
61. *General Comment No 34, Article 19, Freedoms of Opinion and Expression*, United Nations Human Rights Committee, 102nd Session, UN Doc CCPR/C/GC/34, 12 September 2011, at paras 35–36.
62. *Silver v UK (Applications No 5947/72; 6205/73; 7052/75; 7061/75; 7107/75; 7113/75; 7136/75)*, ECtHR, Section Judgment, 25 March 1983.
63. *Silver v UK (Applications No 5947/72; 6205/73; 7052/75; 7061/75; 7107/75; 7113/75; 7136/75)*, ECtHR, Section Judgment, 25 March 1983, at para 97.
64. C Ovey, RCA White and FG Jacobs, *The European Convention on Human Rights* (Oxford UP, Oxford, 2010), at 325.
65. C Ovey, RCA White and FG Jacobs, *The European Convention on Human Rights* (Oxford UP, Oxford, 2010), at 326–27.
66. See, for instance, *Ceylan v Turkey (Application No 23556/94)*, ECtHR, Section Judgment, 8 July 1999; *Incal v Turkey (Application No 41/1997/825/1031)*, ECtHR, Section Judgment, 9 June 1998; *Arslan v Turkey (Application No 23462/94)* ECtHR, Section Judgment, 8 July 1999. P van Dijk, GJH van Hoof, A van Rijn and L Zwaak (eds), *Theory and Practice of the European Convention on Human Rights* (Intersentia, Antwerp, 2006), at 340–42.
67. *Compulsory Membership in an Association Prescribed by Law for the Practice of Journalism (Arts. 13 and 29 American Convention on Human Rights)*, Advisory Opinion OC-5/85, IACtHR, 13 November 1985, at paras 42–44.
68. *Ibid.*
69. L Burgorgue-Larsen, A Úbeda de Torres and R Greenstein, *The Inter-American Court of Human Rights: Case-Law and Commentary* (Oxford UP, Oxford, New York, 2011), at 541; but also see the many references to the ECtHR in the *Compulsory Membership in Journalist Organizations.*
70. *Case of Herrera-Ulloa v Costa Rica (Preliminary Objections, Merits, Reparations and Costs)*, Judgment IACtHR, 2 July 2004, at para 121.
71. *Ibid.*
72. *Ibid* also referring to the necessity test of the ECtHR.
73. A Legg, *The Margin of Appreciation in International Human Rights Law: Deference and Proportionality* (Oxford UP, Oxford, 2012), at 3–4.
74. *Ireland v UK (Application No 5310/71)*, ECtHR, Judgment, Plenary, 18 January 1978.
75. Spielmann (2012), at 4–5.
76. Y Arai-Takahashi, *The Margin of Appreciation Doctrine and the Principle of Proportionality in the Jurisprudence of the ECHR* (Intersentia, Antwerp, Oxford, 2002); at 2–7.
77. G Letsas, "Two Concepts of the Margin of Appreciation" (2006) 26(4) *Oxford J of Legal Studies* 705–32.
78. G Letsas, "Two Concepts of the Margin of Appreciation" (2006) 26(4) *Oxford J of Legal Studies* 705–32, at 706.
79. G Letsas, "Two Concepts of the Margin of Appreciation" (2006) 26(4) *Oxford J of Legal Studies* 705–32.

80. HLL Hill, "Universality versus Subsidiarity: A Reply" (1998) 1 *European Human Rights Law Rev* 73–81, at 75.
81. Dissenting Opinion of Judge De Meyer, *Z v Finland (Application No 22009/93)*, ECtHR, Section Judgment, 25 February 1997.
82. Y Arai-Takahashi, "The Margin of Appreciation Doctrine: A Theoretical Analysis of Strasbourg's Variable Geometry", in A. Føllesdal, G. Ulfstein and B. Peters (eds), *Constituting Europe: The European Court of Human Rights in a National, European and Global Context* (Cambridge UP, Cambridge, 2013) 62–105.
83. J Brauch, "The Margin of Appreciation and the Jurisprudence of the European Court of Human Rights: Threat to the Rule of Law" (2005) 11 *Columbia J of European Law* 113–50.
84. Spielmann (2012).
85. See for instance the Concurring Opinion of Judge Rozakis and the Dissenting opinion of Judge Malinverni in the *Lautsi* judgment, *Lautsi v Italy, Application No 30814/06*, ECtHR, Grand Chamber, 18 March 2011.
86. For a more detailed list see Spielman (2012), at 3, footnote 8.
87. *Case of Ricardo Canese v Paraguay (Merits, Reparations and Costs)*, Judgment IACtHR, 31 August 2004.
88. *Ibid* paras 96–97.
89. For a contrary opinion see A Legg, *The Margin of Appreciation in International Human Rights Law: Deference and Proportionality* (Oxford UP, Oxford, 2012).
90. *Länsman v Finland, Communication No 511/1992*, UN Doc CCPR/C/52/D/511/1992, 8 November 1994.
91. *Ibid* para 9.4
92. *See* for instance the Brighton declaration and its urging of the inclusion of the phrase margin of appreciation in the preamble to the Convention, Section B – Interaction Between the Court and National Authorities, High Level Conference on the Future of the European Court of Human Rights, Brighton Declaration, 20 April 2012 (available at http://hub.coe.int/20120419-brighton-declaration last visited 23 Sep. 13).
93. HLL Hill, "Universality versus Subsidiarity: A Reply" (1998) 1 *European Human Rights Law Rev* 73–81, at 75; J Brauch, "The Margin of Appreciation and the Jurisprudence of the European Court of Human Rights: Threat to the Rule of Law" (2005) 11 *Columbia J of European Law* 113–50; and Y Arai-Takahashi, "The Margin of Appreciation Doctrine: A Theoretical Analysis of Strasbourg's Variable Geometry", in A. Føllesdal, G. Ulfstein and B. Peters (eds), *Constituting Europe: The European Court of Human Rights in a National, European and Global Context* (Cambridge UP, Cambridge, 2013), 62–105.
94. *Handyside v United Kingdom, (Application No 5493/72)*, Section judgment, ECtHR, 7 December 1976, para 49.
95. *Handyside v United Kingdom, (Application No 5493/72)*, Section judgment, ECtHR, 7 December 1976.
96. *Handyside v United Kingdom, (Application No 5493/72)*, Section judgment, ECtHR, 7 December 1976.
97. J Tasioulas, "Human Rights, Legitimacy, and International Law" (2013) 58(1) *American J of Jurisprudence* 1–25.
98. *Case of Usón Ramírez v Venezuela (Preliminary Objections, Merits, Reparations, and Costs)*, Judgment IACtHR, 20 November 2009, at para 83.
99. *Compulsory Membership in an Association Prescribed by Law for the Practice of Journalism (Arts. 13 and 29 American Convention on Human Rights)*, Advisory Opinion OC-5/85, IACtHR, 13 November 1985, at paras 70–71.
100. *Case of Herrera-Ulloa v Costa Rica (Preliminary Objections, Merits, Reparations and Costs)*, Judgment IACtHR, 2 July 2004, at para 116.
101. *General Comment No 34, Article 19, Freedoms of Opinion and Expression*, United Nations Human Rights Committee, 102nd Session, UN Doc CCPR/C/GC/34, 12 September 2011, at paras 2–3.
102. *General Comment No 34, Article 19, Freedoms of Opinion and Expression*, United Nations Human Rights Committee, 102nd Session, UN Doc CCPR/C/GC/34, 12 September 2011, at para 5.
103. *General Comment No 34, Article 19, Freedoms of Opinion and Expression*, United Nations Human Rights Committee, 102nd Session, UN Doc CCPR/C/GC/34, 12 September 2011, at para 2
104. *General Comment No 34, Article 19, Freedoms of Opinion and Expression*, United Nations Human Rights Committee, 102nd Session, UN Doc CCPR/C/GC/34, 12 September 2011.

105. *General Comment No 34, Article 19, Freedoms of Opinion and Expression*, United Nations Human Rights Committee, 102nd Session, UN Doc CCPR/C/GC/34, 12 September 2011.
106. *General Comment No 34, Article 19, Freedoms of Opinion and Expression*, United Nations Human Rights Committee, 102nd Session, UN Doc CCPR/C/GC/34, 12 September 2011.
107. One question that I would like to pose that is not relevant to the task of this article, is that while certainly reasoning is one of the hallmarks of a human being, one can think of societies where the expression of ideas is anything but free and those societies can still exist.
108. *Observer & Guardian v UK (Application No 13585/88)*, Section Judgment, ECtHR, 26 November 1991.
109. *Observer & Guardian v UK (Application No 13585/88)*, Section Judgment, ECtHR, 26 November 1991, at paras 61–70.
110. Just as an example, the ICCPR has been signed and ratified by nations as diverse as all of the EU nations, United States of America, as well as Iran, Iraq, Egypt, India, while China is a signatory but has not ratified it.

Comparative Freedom of Assembly and the Fragmentation of International Human Rights Law

Orsolya Salát

Assuming that the issue of fragmentation of international human rights law can also be usefully examined in the case-law on particular rights using a comparative method, this article examines the divergence and convergence of freedom of assembly guarantees and jurisprudence in international fora. It finds that some identified divergences in fact point to underlying common concerns and assumptions about assemblies. On this basis, the article argues that the fragmentation discourse is prone to structurally analogous, though "reverse", fallacies as the methodology of comparative law. In particular, the functionalist method is much criticised for being apologetic or trapped within one's own conceptual and institutional system, a concern which might be present in the fragmentation debate as well. The article concludes on this basis by formulating some suggestions which might be applied to examining fragmentation in international human rights law and potentially beyond.

I. Introduction

This article examines freedom of assembly clauses and case-law of international forums in order to identify possible divergences and convergences in the level of international human rights protection, and thereby strives to add a complementary dimension to the debate of fragmentation in international law without engaging with the fragmentation literature per se. It is thus assumed that comparative law might contribute to this debate on international law. By comparing the specific human rights jurisprudence of different international conventions and their quasi-judicial bodies, notably the ICCPR, the ECHR, the ACHPR and the ACHR, the following is an inquiry into institutional fragmentation. It examines whether different institutions interpreting different texts produce a different level of human rights protection in analogous factual situations. Fragmentation is therefore understood to arise already from the sole fact of different institutions pronouncing differently on similar cases, i.e. not only when different institutions or regimes might clash, conflict or interact. This understanding of the concept of fragmentation is justified in the realm of human rights law, as different human rights treaties share a commitment to the Universal Declaration of Human Rights.

Freedom of assembly was chosen as it is a right proclaimed in the Universal Declaration and guaranteed in all major human rights treaties, thus it is suitable in principle for testing the phenomenon of fragmentation. It is also a right exercised, abused, and suppressed intensely all around the world. These two factors on their own merit much more scholarly attention than freedom of assembly usually receives.

Furthermore, a specificity of freedom of assembly is that it does not have such extensive case-law as its cognate right, freedom of expression. This is because courts often reconfigure assembly issues into expression issues. Consequently, freedom of assembly also attracts relatively little attention from comparative law scholars. Freedom of assembly lacks any grand doctrine or systematic theory even in domestic courts (except maybe the German Federal Constitutional Court[1]) and in domestic scholarship. It might thus be useful to compare this study's perspective with the results of Ajevski's freedom of expression paper elsewhere in this issue. The certainly incomplete, or comparatively thin, jurisprudential corpus of freedom of assembly on its own might contribute in different ways to the fragmentation discourse from, for instance, case-law on freedom of expression, religion, equal treatment or fair trial rights. Notably, in the case of an undersystematised, undertheorised, in short, understudied right there is much less opportunity for the migration or transplanting of legal doctrines, standards, interpretive ideas, etc. than there might be in the case of a more widely researched right and its case-law. In contrast, the commonalities revealed in the case of freedom of assembly might be more profound than the apparent similarities between other rights might suggest.

After a short overview of the guarantee provisions in the text of the European, American and African regional conventions and the ICCPR (section 1), this article examines a few assembly characteristic issues of interpretation which have arisen in some decisions of both the ECtHR and the Human Rights Committee (HRC) (section 2). The ECtHR has for the last two decades increasingly elaborated a significant jurisprudence on freedom of assembly, while the HRC has only a few related communications. The Inter-American Court of Human Rights has not handed down any decision on freedom of assembly. The African Court of Human and People's Rights has lately issued its very first decision[2] on the merits but the case was not about freedom of assembly.

The approach taken in this article is to examine only those questions which have arisen both in the HRC and at the ECtHR, while it is also telling that the Inter-American system, certainly on a continent with very lively protest movements, has not yet ruled on freedom of assembly. The assumption is therefore that the level of fragmentation ought to be examined only in areas which are actually problematised in these jurisdictions. These common areas are likely to expand in the future as the jurisprudential corpus grows. However, for now, the freedom of assembly issues which emerge as commonly significant in both of these jurisdictions can be reduced to three questions: (i) the peacefulness requirement as a determinant of the scope of the right to assembly (section 2.1); (ii) the question of advance notice or permit (section 2.2); and (iii) the relationship between freedom of assembly and freedom of expression, the most confounding conceptual issue in the area of expressive rights (section 2.3).

The concluding section assesses the particular divergences and convergences found, and also provides a broader assessment in light of the fragmentation claim. It concludes, at least in relation to freedom of assembly – and contrary to the suggestion of the introductory study – that it is not necessarily the divergence of doctrines, tests, and justifications,[3] let alone texts, but outcomes and underlying assumptions that matter for the purposes of fragmentation scrutiny. Furthermore, the fact that it is – though substantively an article on international human rights law – methodologically a comparative law exercise, shows up potentially fruitful further questions for research in the field of the fragmentation of international law. I conclude with a general suggestion that scholarship about this fragmentation could benefit from methodological debates in comparative law, and it might be especially warranted to use the critique of functionalism in comparative law as "an inverted mirror" in which the potential fallacies and overreach of the fragmentation approach might be more easily identified.

II. Texts

The provisions of the conventions on freedom of assembly are reproduced in Table 1.

III. Similarities: Structure, Aims, Derogation

The texts of three assembly guarantees (ECHR, ICCPR, ACHR) are similar in that the scope of freedom of assembly covers only peaceful assemblies, which means that non-peaceful assemblies are not protected. Exactly what that means will be clarified below. The Banjul Charter does not mention peacefulness in the guarantee of freedom of assembly.

Common limits are also to be found in the texts, for example, that the treaties only allow restrictions which are "necessary in a democratic society" (in the African instrument, only "necessary") in the interests of certain legitimate aims. The structure of international human rights norms is thus clearly converging. Among the listed aims common to all four documents are national security, public safety, the protection of health or morals, and protection of rights and freedoms of others.

Finally, none of the examined conventions considers freedom of assembly a non-derogable right, it is included neither in ECHR, article 15, ACHR, article 27(2) nor ICCPR, article 4.

IV. Differences

Formulations of the guarantee

Concerning the guarantee of the right to assembly, the ECHR, similar to the UDHR, proclaims that "everyone has the right to freedom of peaceful assembly", the Banjul Charter, article 11 states that every individual has the right to "assemble freely with others", while in the ICCPR and the ACHR "the right of peaceful assembly shall be recognized." This latter formulation implies a weaker obligation[4] than the others. Apart from this difference, the ACHR adds "without arms" to "peaceful", which is similar to the formulation of, for example the German Basic Law, article 8.

Limits of the right (lawfulness and legitimate aim of the interference)

As to the form of the restriction, the ECHR and the Banjul Charter require that it be prescribed/provided for by law, while the other conventions only state that the restriction conforms with the law, apparently meaning that administrative decisions having some basis in formal law would also suffice. In practice, however, it is clear that the ECtHR has relaxed this requirement. No formal legislative act is required, but the norm in question has to conform to certain substantive criteria of predictability and foreseeability.[5]

Apart from those mentioned above, legitimate uses of the restriction include the prevention of disorder or crime under the ECHR and public order under the ACHR and the ICCPR. At first sight, the European text appears narrower, but in interpretation the ECtHR relaxes this requirement to the extent that the different textual versions are indistinguishable in practice. There is basically no imminence or immediacy requirement,[6] and the concept of disorder is also widely understood in Strasbourg.[7]

Table 1.

ICCPR: Article 21	ACHR: Article 15	ACHPR: Article 11	ECHR: Article 11
The right of peaceful assembly shall be recognised. No restrictions may be placed on the exercise of this right other than those imposed in conformity with the law and which are necessary in a democratic society in the interests of national security or public safety, public order (*ordre public*), the protection of public health or morals or the protection of the rights and freedoms of others.	The right of peaceful assembly, without arms, is recognised. No restrictions may be placed on the exercise of this right other than those imposed in conformity with the law and necessary in a democratic society in the interest of national security, public safety or public order, or to protect public health or morals or the rights or freedoms of others.	Every individual shall have the right to assemble freely with others. The exercise of this right shall be subject only to necessary restrictions provided for by law in particular those enacted in the interest of national security, the safety, health, ethics and rights and freedoms of others.	Everyone has the right to freedom of peaceful assembly (and to freedom of association with others, including the right to form and to join trade unions for the protection of his interests.) No restrictions shall be placed on the exercise of these rights other than such as are prescribed by law and are necessary in a democratic society in the interests of national security or public safety, for the prevention of disorder or crime, for the protection of health or morals or for the protection of the rights and freedoms of others. This article shall not prevent the imposition of lawful restrictions on the exercise of these rights by members of the armed forces, of the police or of the administration of the State.

Authorisation for restrictions as to the personal scope of freedom of assembly

The ICCPR allows for the imposition of lawful restrictions on members of the armed forces and the police in their exercise of freedom of association (article 22), but not on freedom of assembly (article 21). It does not contain any such authorisation for limiting the political rights of aliens either. ICCPR, article 25 contains some rights for citizens only, however, freedom of assembly is not one of them, so any restriction has to be justified under article 21(2).

The ECHR, article 11 specifically allows "the imposition of lawful restrictions on the exercise of these rights by members of the armed forces, of the police or of the administration of the State." Article 16 states that article 11 does not hinder a state in restricting the political activity of aliens. The ACHR does not contain a specific authorisation to restrict the political rights of aliens, police, or armed forces. The Banjul Charter does not explicitly authorise person-specific restrictions, but arguably the various duties in Chapter II – in future interpretation – might place a heavier burden on groups mentioned in other texts.

V. Fragmentation of Texts – Consumed by Interpretation?

The studied conventions share similarities but differ strikingly in other respects. There is fragmentation even within the substantial differences: for example, in the question of the political rights of aliens, police, and armed forces, applicable standards clearly diverge. Though the ILC report on fragmentation[8] might be taken to be concerned with textual differences, human rights scholars do not appear to be worried about them. This silence signifies a shared understanding that human rights norms are largely immune to a strict textual interpretation, and can be molded according to higher interpretive techniques, such purposive, teleological and dynamic interpretation or the understanding of the convention as a living instrument. In some cases, general (not assembly-specific) interpretation clearly reduces these differences, such as the requirement of "prescribed by law". In other cases – such as specific authorisation to limit the rights of the police, armed forces or foreigners, or with the exclusion of armed assemblies – the rationales behind the specific limits might be easily taken into account in interpretation (in proportionality analysis) even if the text does not explicitly state them. The next section examines to what extent this assumption holds true with regard to selected leading cases.

VI. Interpretation

Fear of particularism, including fragmentation, arises solely from the fact of parallel institutions, regardless of the text. Parallel institutions run the risk of diverging interpretation even where the underlying texts match exactly, and can produce converging interpretation even where the texts are different (perhaps within the bounds of avoiding, at least on the surface, a *contra legem* interpretation).

The IACtHR and the ACtHPR have not ruled on the freedom of assembly so there is no jurisprudence to compare. The ECtHR has an increasing corpus of article 11 case-law, though it also started quite late, and it was actually not until 1991 that it found a violation. The HRC has only a handful of cases under article 21. The jurisdictions, thus, though to a differing extent, share a certain moderation when it comes to freedom of assembly. Freedom of assembly is not at the centre of litigation, despite the fact that assemblies are ongoing all over the world, and it would be absurd to claim, for example, that the European continent clearly experiences more (controversial) assembly activity than its American counterpart.

It is most likely that there are cases on assemblies decided under different rights provisions – prime candidates are right to life, liberty and freedom of expression – in each of the jurisdictions. (Note that none of the freedom of expression cases at the IACtHR involved assemblies.) Here, analogous issues arising under the parallel articles in each convention are compared in order to reach some conclusions as to the fragmentation claim. I shall start the analysis with the ECtHR as it has the most elaborate jurisprudence. This does not imply any preference or priority in terms of substance or quality, but is simply done for reasons of quantity and thickness of jurisprudential layers.

VII. Peaceable and Peaceful as Delimitation of the Scope of the Right

The ECtHR's stance on peacefulness

Article 11, similar to most other national and international instruments, protects only the freedom of peaceful assembly. The ECHR offers substantive review in this regard; the *Stankov*[9] decision at least testifies to such an approach. In this case, the Bulgarian Government argued that the ban on demonstrations organised by the United Macedonian Organisation Ilinden was not an interference since the planned demonstrations would not have been of a peaceful nature. The ECtHR reiterated that article 11 only protects peaceful assemblies, but that a peaceful character is only foregone if the organisers and participants have violent intentions. On the facts of the case, the Government could not reasonably conclude that the planned demonstrations would be non-peaceful. The *Stankov* decision is one example of substantive review which appears to stand in contradiction to several earlier inadmissibility decisions handed down by the Commission. *Chappell*[10] and *Pendragon*,[11] for example, both included complete blanket bans around Stonehenge for the period around the summer solstice. The Commission did not find it problematic that the cause of the danger of disturbance concededly lay outside the sphere of action of the applicants. Therefore, their right to freedom of assembly (and religion) was interfered with without any fault on their part. Remarkably, the Commission did not adhere to the relevant *dicta* of *Plattform "Ärzte für das Leben"*,[12] according to which states are required to take reasonable measures to prevent the violent behavior of others threatening an of itself peaceful assembly. The Chappell–Pendragon line of inadmissibility seems also to conflict with earlier decisions of the Commission itself: in a 1980 case, *CARAF*,[13] it stated that,

> The possibility of violent counter-demonstrations or the possibility of extremists with violent intentions, not members of the organising association, joining the demonstration cannot as such take away that right. Even if there is a real risk of a public procession resulting in disorder by developments outside the control of those organizing it, such procession for this reason alone does not fall out of the scope of Article 11 (1) of the Convention.

In this case, a planned antifascist procession was caught up by the general ban on processions in a certain area of London. The Commission accepted the ban as justified because earlier protests by the National Front had resulted in serious damage to persons and property which even large contingents of police could not prevent. In this case, therefore, the peaceful antifascists were restricted in their assembly rights because of previously non-peaceful others. Unlike in *Chappell* and *Pendragon*, the application was not found to be outside the scope of article 11.

That such an application would be manifestly ill-founded today is confirmed by the *Ezelin*[14] jurisprudence: there the court required that a person be punished only if he himself committed some reprehensible act, which has since been reaffirmed, *e.g.* in *Galstyan v Armenia.*[15] *Ziliberberg v Moldova* is also a case involving a demonstration which gradually turned violent, but where there was no indication that the applicant participated in the violence; he was still fined for participating. The court emphasised that[16]

> an individual does not cease to enjoy the right to peaceful assembly as a result of sporadic violence or other punishable acts committed by others in the course of the demonstration, if the individual in question remains peaceful in his or her own intentions or behaviour.

How sporadic is "Sporadic" is of course open to interpretation, and one should not rush to conclude that such demonstrations can be only dispersed where each and every participant is violent.

On the other hand, under *Plattform "Ärzte für das Leben"*[17] the possibility of violent counter-demonstrations is not a reason to ban a demonstration: "[T]he authorities have a duty to take appropriate measures with regard to lawful demonstrations in order to ensure their peaceful conduct and the safety of all citizens."[18] It is also settled case-law that an unlawful situation does not justify an infringement of freedom of assembly,[19] certainly there is no possibility to interpret non-peacefulness as simple unlawfulness. Furthermore – and unlike in cases of freedom of expression, where *e.g.* Holocaust denial[20] falls under article 17 – abuse of rights does not figure in the jurisprudence. The ECtHR has not ruled that certain viewpoints may in themselves amount to an abuse of the right *to assembly*, or are inherently unpeaceful.[21] This is a question which arose with regard to the ICCPR which is discussed next.

The Human Rights Committee on peacefulness

During the drafting of the ICCPR, there was discussion about the definition of "peaceful", and whether it should be changed to "peaceable" (*pacifique* or *paisible* in French, compare also "the right of the people peaceably to assemble" in the First Amendment to the US constitution).

This relates to the question of whether peacefulness is a substantive or a modal question. As mentioned above, the ECtHR clearly understands it as a question of modality: the (intention of) violence has to be overwhelming for the assembly to lose its peaceful character, independent of the theme or the political stance of the participants.

During the drafting process of the ICCPR, the Soviet Union wanted to exclude assemblies (or any activities) of fascist or antidemocratic movements from the protection.[22] This approach was rejected, however, and no specific substantive stance lies outside the protection of article 21.

In accordance with the modal approach, the HRC urged the Russian Federation (in 2003) to revise its law on "extremist activities" for being too vague to comply with article 21.[23] Similarly, with regard to Hong Kong, the Committee criticised the definition of treason and sedition for being too vague with reference to article 21.[24]

The positive obligation of the state to protect the peaceful character of an assembly – especially against violent counter-demonstrators or the provocation of others, including the police – is also recognised by the HRC.[25]

Again, similar to the ECtHR (see *Ezelin v France*, above), the HRC imposes the principle of individual responsibility in a different formulation: with regard to Canada, it stated[26] that

> the State party should ensure that the right of persons to peacefully participate in social protests is respected, and ensure that only those committing criminal offences during demonstrations are arrested.

This formulation shows that it is individual participation that can be peaceful or non-peaceful, the assembly as such is not a homogeneous unit of reference.

Fragmented in peace

In sum, there is consensus under both the ECHR and the ICCPR that assemblies which lose their peaceful character do not fall under the scope of protection of the right to assembly, and thus can be limited without fulfilling the justification requirements in article 11(2) and article 21(2).

There is also a tendency in both jurisdictions to narrow those cases which render an assembly non-peaceful, thus depriving it of human rights protection. Both jurisdictions recognise the positive obligation of the state to protect the peaceful character of an assembly. In different terms, in effect both the HRC and the ECHR uphold the principle of individual responsibility with regard to assemblies considered non-peaceful and those upon which sanctions can be imposed.

VIII. Prior Notice or Permit: Restriction, Determinance of Scope, and Exceptions

The ECtHR appears not to consider that the requirement of prior notice or a permit might be a restriction on the right to freedom of assembly.[27] Notice or the application for a permit is seen as a tool to realise the state's positive obligation to secure freedom of assembly or enabling an assembly to occur, or even "not to use powers that [the police] may validly have (for instance, of regulating traffic) to obstruct the event."[28]

However, this does not prevent the court from gradually carving out some reasonable exemptions from the notice requirement. It requires states not to disperse assemblies for the sole reason of their being unnotified,[29] and acknowledges the right to spontaneous or "urgent" demonstrations, at least as an immediate response to a political event.[30]

The HRC, on the other hand, appears to consider prior notice or a permit to be a restriction for the purposes of article 21 inquiry, but it accepts that it may be justified. In the leading case on article 21, *Kivenmaa v Finland*, the Committee explicitly contemplates that "a requirement to notify the police of an intended demonstration in a public place six hours before its commencement may be compatible with the permitted limitations laid down in article 21 of the Covenant."[31] Thus advance notice is clearly considered an interference with the right.

In a case against Russia, the Committee found that serial denials of permission to hold a picket at different suggested locations were in violation of article 21.[32] In a case against Belarus, a former opposition leader successfully argued that the non-issuance of a lawyer's licence because of participation at an unauthorised, but peaceful, rally violated both his right to freedom of expression and to freedom of assembly.[33] Though the Committee did not examine the authorisation requirement, it concluded that the sanctions imposed on the applicant were not justified or necessary for either freedom of expression or freedom of assembly.

Thus, despite the fact that the Committee does not operate a spontaneous demonstration clause, it might arrive at the same conclusion as the ECtHR, especially when the notice system is misused by government. In effect, in these cases the violation lies in abusively denying a permit or disproportionately sanctioning the holding of an assembly without prior notice or permit.[34] These are exactly the concerns animating the decisions in *Oya Ataman & Bukta* at the ECtHR.

Another way of avoiding the burdens flowing from assembly laws in both jurisdictions is the pronouncement of the applicability of freedom of expression instead of freedom of assembly, as will be discussed next.

IX. Conceptual Issues: The Relation to Freedom of Expression

Conceptualities and, more specifically, the relation between freedom of expression and freedom of assembly are neuralgic questions in every jurisdiction aware enough to take these rights seriously. The following comparison should thus be seen as providing a snapshot at the crossroads of institutional fragmentation and the overlap of the scope of rights ("Grundrechtskonkurrenz").

X. The ECtHR on the Relation between Assembly and Expression

The ECtHR only lately contended explicitly that the freedom of assembly, just as its twin-right of association in article 11,[35] has an autonomous meaning under the Convention.[36] The Commission has already noted, and the court has since embraced as a constant reference that "freedom of assembly covers both private meetings and meetings in public thoroughfares as well as static meetings and public processions;"[37] it can be exercised both by individuals and those organising the assembly.[38] Most probably, however, it does not cover *ad hoc* or accidental gatherings of people without a purpose, or for purely social purposes.[39]

Protests and direct action where only one or a few participants appear are covered by the freedom of expression right of article 10.[40] Article 11 is in general considered *lex specialis* to article 10, thus article 10 doctrine can always apply to assemblies, while the connection is not valid the other way around.

Contrary to some national jurisdictions (notably the United States[41] and Germany[42]), the ECtHR does not apply any modality doctrine which would allow for greater restriction on the "form" of expression (including forms of assembly, such as marching or other conduct) than on their "content" or "substance". In relation to the press, the court declared in 1991 that "not only the substance of the ideas and information expressed, but also the form in which they are conveyed" is protected by Article 10.[43] In 2009, the court expressly applied this doctrine to an assembly advocating reproductive rights on a boat off the Portuguese shore which was prevented from entering territorial waters by a war vessel. A demonstration held on a boat in the territorial waters of a state was considered by the court to be a "mode of diffusion of information and ideas", restrictions on which, in certain situations, "can affect in an essential manner, the substance of the information and ideas in question."[44]

In these cases, the ECtHR is thus unequivocally clear about the meaning generating function of the modalities (be they of assemblies or of other expressive activities). Nevertheless, the court recently contended that "even otherwise protected expression is not equally permissible in all places and all times."[45] "Interference ... might be legitimate when the particular place and time of the otherwise protected expression unequivocally changes the *meaning* of a certain display."[46] Thus, context and circumstances matter. The case of *Fáber v Hungary* concerned the removal, detention and administrative fine resulting from the display of an Arpad-striped flag (an old Hungarian flag used by the arrow cross movement in World War 2) at a site where Jews were murdered in great numbers by the Danube in Budapest during World War 2. The court found article 11 (including notice requirement) inapplicable, but found a violation of article 10. Notably, the removal of the flag could not be justified under any provisions of para 2, as it was a lawfully displayed flag with multiple meanings and, in the present case, was not used to identify with a totalitarian regime.

Another recent decision against Hungary implies a clear distinction between expression and assembly for the purposes of fundamental rights restriction. The case involved a two-person performance beside the Hungarian Parliament consisting of hanging out several items of cloths on a fence, symbolising the Nation's "dirty laundry", in protest against the political crisis ongoing since 2006. The performance lasted only a few minutes, was followed by a dialogue with journalists, and then ended. The performers were later fined for "abuse of freedom of assembly" as they had not notified their "demonstration". The court dismissed the government's argument that the performance was to qualify as an assembly, which falls under the assembly law, and can be subjected to a requirement of prior notice. On the contrary, the ECtHR doubted that such a short two-person "event could have generated the gathering of a significant crowd warranting specific measure on the side of the authorities."[47] Had the specific measure been warranted, freedom of assembly (instead or alongside freedom of expression) would have been applicable, which would have allowed for the imposition of a notification requirement.[48] By requiring advance notice for the 13-minute, 2-person performance, however, "[t]he national authorities' approach to the concept of assembly does not correspond to the rationale of the notification rule."[49] The rationale of the notification rule is the effective coordination and facilitation of assembly, the prevention of public disorder or the protection of the rights of others. The lack of these specific concerns rendered the short, 2-person performance under article 10 instead of article 11. This confirms the fall-back nature of article 10 (or the *lex specialis* status of article 11) as developed in earlier case-law, and implies that for the assembly law to "kick in" some additional, specific concerns are required. In this regard, freedom of assembly is considered a freedom of expression discounted by the mentioned police powers, a kind of "freedom of expression minus".

This view is strengthened by another already mentioned, otherwise very much rights protective decision from 2009.[50] In this case, a vessel providing information about abortion and family planning ("*Women on Waves*") was denied entry to the territorial waters of Portugal. The ECtHR found the issue best and sufficiently examined under Article 10, because the principal grievance consisted of the denial of "their right to inform the public about their stance on abortion and women's rights in general." (§ 28) The court explicitly stated that article 10 "protects equally the mode of diffusion of ideas and opinions" (§30).

In sum, it appears that the ECHR (i) is willing to recognise the expressive potential of the "modalities" of an assembly, but that (ii) it still might allow heavier or different restrictions on assemblies than on speech, if those restrictions correspond to the additional externalities of assemblies.

XI. Relation of Assembly and Expression under the HRC Jurisprudence

The HRC appears also somewhat confused over the issue of the relation of articles 19 and 21, freedom of expression and freedom of assembly. The Committee sometimes rejected the assembly claim, but declared the claim admissible under freedom of expression.

Coleman v Australia involved a condemnation for taking part in a public address (a one-person political speech in a mall of about 15–20 minutes' duration) without prior written permit from the town council.[51] The complainant argued that the conviction violated article 21 and article 19. The HRC declared the article 21 part of the complaint was inadmissible for lack of substantiation, but found a violation of article 19, for unnecessary restriction.

In one of its few cases on article 21, *Kivenmaa v Finland*, the HRC faced the question of a "protest in a cheering crowd", i.e. a situation where a minority in an audience engaged in a protest performance while the others were merely onlookers of an event against which the complainants protested. Ms. Kivenmaa, together with 25 other members of the Social Democratic Youth Association, went into a crowd gathering next to the Presidential Palace on the occasion of a visit of a foreign head of state. They distributed leaflets and raised a banner critical of the human rights record of the visiting head of state. She was charged with holding a public meeting without prior notice. Domestic courts found that Ms. Kivenmaa's group was distinguishable from the crowd, and thus she could be considered to have organised a public meeting. She claimed, among others, that articles 19 and 21 ICCPR have been violated. The Committee, though not denying that the requirement of notice for a demonstration may be justified, found "*evident* from the information provided by the parties that the gathering of several individuals at the site of the welcoming ceremonies for a foreign head of State on an official visit, publicly announced in advance by the State party authorities, cannot be regarded as a demonstration" (emphasis added).

The claim of the state, that displaying a banner turned the presence of Ms. Kivenmaa's group into a demonstration, was rejected by the Committee with the argument "that any restrictions upon the right to assemble must fall within the limitation provisions of article 21. A requirement to pre-notify a demonstration would normally be for reasons of national security or public safety, public order, the protection of public health or morals or the protection of the rights and freedoms of others. Consequently, the application of Finnish legislation on demonstrations to such a gathering cannot be considered as an application of a restriction permitted by article 21 of the Covenant" (§9.2).

This reasoning is, at the very least, unclear, if not manifestly incomprehensible and illogical.[52] At the very least, the Committee should have accepted that it was a demonstration and that, as such, it might be subject to six hours' notice, but in this case the notice requirement was not necessary, or that – as the ECtHR sometimes rules – the lack of notice did not authorise the dispersal of the demonstration, or the prevention of Ms. Kivenmaa continuing her protest, including raising the banner. Bidault speculates that considerations of non-discrimination might have animated the Committee not to accept that the protesters were a demonstration.[53] I would further translate these as concerns over content neutrality which disprove additional burdens flowing from the categorisation of being an assembly, while the others, of an opposing mindset, are only categorised as spectators, spared from any administrative burden.

Different doctrine, similar assumption

Before forming more determinate conclusions on the background considerations which might have animated the curious (and sparse) reasoning in *Kivenmaa*, a parallel case at the ECtHR is worth examining. *Chorherr v Austria* is factually analogous, though it did not turn on conceptual issues in relation to speech, and was considered solely under the free expression guarantee – what often and tellingly happens to assemblies. The case involved a military parade where applicants went in with placards and leaflets to protest against Austria's acquisition of interceptor fighter planes. Pacifists slightly interfered with the view of a few parade-watchers, causing some commotion among the spectators (though if they moved away, they could see fully). Applicants were removed from the scene, and later convicted for administrative offences against public decency and breach of the peace. They claimed violation of article 10 at Strasbourg, and did not invoke freedom of assembly at all. The ECtHR found that the restriction fell within the margin of appreciation, and was considered non-excessive to the potential disturbance Mr. Chorherr "must have realised", and also because the measures were imposed in order "to prevent breaches of the peace and not [in order] to frustrate the expression of an opinion."[54]

In my view, it could be credibly argued that this is exactly what happened in the case of Ms. Kivenmaa: she was clearly singled out for expression of a specific opinion. Of course, *Chorherr* would have been likely to have turned out differently following the Arpad flag decision at the ECtHR. Nonetheless, if the pacifists were genuinely removed not for their views, but for the commotion they caused, then maybe that which looks so different from so many viewpoints underlies a very similar consideration. If you are harassed for your opinion, then it is a violation of your free expression rights, and that violation should not be covered up and argued away in the disguise of freedom of assembly, with its potentially more extensive permissible limits (such as the requirement of prior notice). However, if you are held responsible for the consequences of your behavior, your expression rights are not violated.

On the other hand, the *Coleman* case of the HRC, involving a one-person public address, is analogous to the ECtHR decision discussed above (the Nation's "dirty laundry performance"). The assembly claim of Mr. Coleman was dismissed, while the Hungarian government's argument relying on freedom of assembly was also rejected in the "dirty laundry performance" case. Whether or not the HRC did something different in the Coleman case than the ECHR did in the "dirty laundry performance" case depends on our perspective, or, more precisely, how distanced we are when we look at the decisions. The diverging approach to the assembly claims can be either considered (i) a difference arising out of institutional fragmentation; or (ii) a wholly innocent contingency of the complaints – in one case explicitly referring to freedom of assembly next to freedom of expression, and not in the other; or (iii) a wholly innocent contingency of divergent regulation: the Queensland town requires a permit even for a one-person public addresses, while in the Hungarian case, quite to the contrary, notice could only be required if something could be qualified as an "assembly." All these differences and contingencies however do not account for – but rather disguise – the similarity of concerns motivating the overlapping outcome, i.e. violation of freedom of expression.

XII. Elusivity of the Debate or Elusivity of the Subject: The Comparative Lawyer's Interpreting "Fragmentation"

From this short and in fact fragmented inquiry, four particular technical conclusions arise as to divergence and convergence.

First, with regard to the text of the guarantees in the different jurisdictions, there are partial overlaps but also some significant differences. None of them appears really to give reason to worry, in the same way as differences in constitutional texts.[55] Secondly, regarding the criterion of peacefulness, the jurisdictions basically display an identical interpretation, though of course the individual assessment might differ from one case to another just as it might in the opinion of a majority and dissenting judge.

In contrast, there are very clear doctrinal differences with regard to prior notice. The ECtHR does not consider it to be a restriction, while the HRC does. The ECtHR carves out exemptions from notice even while staying within article 11, while the HRC does not. Finally, as to the relation between freedom of assembly and freedom of expression, the two bodies again appear to argue very differently.

These four observations are anything but revealing for a trained eye in human rights law. The banal differences and similarities either affect the legal situation of persons or they do not. Nothing, or almost nothing, follows from them regarding the level of rights protection granted in a particular jurisdiction. The human rights scholar could, on this basis, tell not much more to the international law scholar than that the question of fragmentation is a gradual one in human rights law. Certainly there are some divergences, but they do not seem to be so overwhelming as to question the integrity of the human rights system. Alternatively, there certainly are convergences, but they do not seem to be so overwhelming as to demonstrate the unity of the human rights system. Such a conclusion, true as it is, does not provide much added value to the fragmentation discourse.

Instead, the reasons for this state of affairs need to be explained and reflected upon. As a result, the following more general considerations can be drawn from this short inquiry on the freedom of assembly.

To some extent, the divergences are technical, which might not greatly affect the actual enjoyment of the right in question. Such is the case with whether prior notice is a restriction or not, or whether the wearing of arms at an assembly qualifies that single armed participant immediately as non-peaceful, or not until the court has examined the justification, etc. The sort of fragmentation which raises concern would be a divergence in the level of rights protection in the final outcome of a case, i.e. where one could establish that a claimant would be better off had she turned to the other organ (as it was to be feared in the Norwegian religious education cases[56]). On the basis of the present inquiry, no such threat lingers over the freedom of assembly, though of course that could change any moment.

More interestingly, paradoxically, such divergences might bring to light hidden or unconscious but shared assumptions which are formulated in different ways in different jurisdictions.

In my view, this happens with freedom of expression. In fact, the stances the ECtHR and the HRC take on this issue do not have much in common on the surface of their arguments. Nonetheless, in both jurisdictions, these different arguments highlight the same problem, although invisible from within the jurisdiction: whether freedom of assembly is a "freedom of expression-minus" or a self-standing, independent right. This is a slightly more visible issue (but still not explicit) in the context of the First Amendment, where scholars talk about a neglected or forgotten right to freedom of assembly.[57] Consider the "speech plus" doctrine,[58] where the additional element to speech (the "plus") merits a "minus" in the strength of protection.[59] From a theoretical angle, some authors argue to the contrary that freedom of assembly does not merit protection alongside freedom of expression,[60] in accordance with the fears of much early crowd psychology from Le Bon to Freud.[61] Therefore, looking at human rights jurisprudence through the lens of fragmentation might actually enhance our knowledge and reflection on the problematic nature of a specific human right.

On the other hand, this exercise about the right to freedom of assembly might be symptomatic of the limits of theorising on the fragmentation of human rights law in general: the fact that there are no cases at the IACtHR, very few at the HRC, and many, but only recently, at the ECtHR might be taken as cautionary signs that the fragmentation discourse is not to be forgetful about the methodological dangers of unreflected comparison. Maybe international law could learn from the intense debates around the methodology of comparative law. International law, especially international human rights law, in fact, aspires to something similar to what the first methodologically conscious comparatist, Saleilles attributed to comparative law: a "droit idéal relative", which, if properly elaborated, reveals a "droit commun de l'humanité civilisée".[62] A further step in the history of comparative law aims to explicitly dispense with the sole focus on texts and formal legal rules and look for the functions that law fulfills.[63]. Fully-fledged functionalism is, however, criticised for being apologetic of or being trapped within one's own system or culture, or simply for misconstruing an ideal function.[64] Applied to fragmentation in international law, it can be hypothesised that those working within one regime or institution will transpose their own texts, concepts and rules to other regimes or institutions, which contributes to the appearance of fragmentation. It does not follow of course that there exists no real fragmentation, just as it is surely possible to formulate and research adequately some of the functions that law fulfills in every society. In some cases, however, what looks like legal fragmentation might on closer inspection turn out to be the result of factual differences, of erratic assumptions about common social problems or their weight, sheer (though inspiring) doctrinal differences having no bearing on the actual level of human rights protection, though surely they can be as they appear: true legal divergences. Certainly this plethora of results is the lesson from this inquiry regarding freedom of assembly. This might suggest that the fallacies of fragmentation discourse might be the opposite of the concerns with comparative law: comparative lawyers tend (or at least used to, classically, e.g. Zweigert and Kötz[65]) to see similarity and construct unity everywhere, while fragmentationists overemphasise differences and tensions. However, logically, the reverse might be true, too, but of course on a different level: ostentatious similarities, tests, doctrines, and arguments copied might in fact be only covers for divergences, legitimising the particular decision a given organ wishes to take (see, e.g., again from comparative law, Kahn-Freund or Vörös[66]). Alternatively, one regime might for some reason resist the smooth integration of a doctrine, test or justification seemingly identically present in another regime, and start to distort it in order to fit into its own logic (*mutatis mutandis*, Somek[67]). These are questions and possibilities which might potentially bear fruit when (trans)posed and examined with regard to particular issues in the fragmentation discourse of international law.

In sum, I hope to have shown through the example of freedom of assembly in this article that fragmentation discourse, if it is to be expanded into international human rights law, certainly ought take into account a wide range of intermingling contextual elements (*e.g.* at least in the sense of a "reverse" or inverted neofunctionalism[68]). These include not only the human rights texts (at the least), applied doctrines, standards, justifications, particular facts of the cases, and outcomes of decisions, but also – as we have seen – domestic regulations, and procedural strategies of the applicant and government alike.

However, this might drive the debate into another impasse well-known from (and unresolved in) comparative law. Just as comparative law is not really self-confident about where its subject starts and ends (both vertically and horizontally), studying international law from the perspective of fragmentation also makes the boundaries of international law – at least international human rights law – look uncertain. An inverted comparative law methodological awareness spills into the problem of vanishing boundaries of the subject, international law itself, as what is traditionally understood as domestic law and legal culture might need to be taken into account as well. That might be the price to be paid for the avoidance of some errors due to increased self-reflection.

Notes

1. *BVerfGE 69, 315* ("Brokdorf"), 1985.
2. African Court of Human & Peoples' Rights, *Tanganyika Law Society et al. v United Republic of Tanzania*, Application Nos 09/2011 and 11/2011. Judgment of 14 June 2013.
3. See Adjevski, this issue.
4. M Nowak, *UN Covenant on Civil and Political Rights: CCPR Commentary* (Kehl, NP Engel, 2005), at 392.
5. See, e.g., *Djavit An v Turkey*, Application No 20652/92. Judgment of 20 February 2003, §65 (finding a violation for non-foreseeability).
6. D Mead, *The New Law of Peaceful Protest. Rights and Regulations in the Human Rights Act Era* (Hart Publishing, Oxford, 2010), at 361.
7. For instance, the legitimate aim of preventing disorder qualified the unhindered flow of traffic in a pedestrian area or avoiding excessive noise in Commission decisions (*GS v Austria*, Application No 14923/89. Decision on admissibility of 30 November 1992, *S v Austria*, Application No 13812/88. Decision on admissibility of 3 December 1990). The court, in a similar vein, accepted the enforced evacuation of a church occupied by protestors with the consent of religious authorities (*Cisse v France*, Application No 51346/99. Judgment of 9 April 2002), similar to a retrospective disciplinary sanction, imposed after the assembly was long over (*Ezelin v France*, Application No 11800/85. Judgment of 26 April 1991, Series A No 202) as measures pursuing the prevention of disorder.
8. M Koskenniemi, *Report on Fragmentation of International Law: Difficulties Arising from the Diversification and Expansion of International Law* (International Law Commission, UN Doc. A/CN.4/L.682, 2006).
9. *Stankov and the United Macedonian Organisation Ilinden v Bulgaria*, Application Nos 29221/95, 29225/95. Judgment of 2 October 2001.
10. *Chappell v United Kingdom*, Application No 12587/86. Admissibility decision of 14 July 1987.
11. *Pendragon v United Kingdom*, Application No 31416/96. Admissibility decision of 19 October 1998.
12. *Plattform "Ärzte für das Leben" v Austria*, Application No 10126/82. Judgment of 21 June 1988.
13. *Christians against Racism & Fascism (CARAF) v United Kingdom*, Application No 8440/78. Admissibility decision of 16 July 1980.
14. *Ezelin v France*, Application No 11800/85. Judgment of 26 April 1991.
15. *Galstyan v Armenia*, Application No 26986/03. Judgment of 15 November 2007.
16. *Ziliberberg v Moldova*, Application No 61821/00. Admissibility decision of 4 May 2004.
17. *Plattform "Ärzte für das Leben" v Austria, supra* note 12.
18. *Oya Ataman v Turkey*, Application No 74552/01. Judgment of 5 December 2006 at §35.
19. *Oya Ataman v Turkey*, §39, referring to *Cisse v France*, Application No 51346/99. Judgment of 9 April 2002, §50.
20. E.g. §53, *Lehideux & Isorni v France*, Application No 55/1997/839/1045. Judgment of 23 September 1998.
21. A close case is though the French "Gallic soup" demonstration, *Association Solidarité des Francais v France*, No 26787/07. Admissibility decision of 16 June 2011. Even there, however, the court found that the discriminatory message of the demonstrators would cause disturbances to public order, and this latter fact mandated the finding of inadmissibility (manifestly ill-founded). Thus, the message was not qualified as unpeaceful, thus falling outside article 11, nor abusive of the right to assembly, falling under article 17.
22. M Nowak, *UN Covenant on Civil and Political Rights: CCPR Commentary* (Kehl, NP Engel, 2005), at 372; M Bidault, *Article 21 in Le pacte international relatif aux droits civils et politiques; commentaire article par article* (E. Decaux, Paris, Economica, 2010), at 476.
23. M Bidault, *Article 21 in Le pacte international relatif aux droits civils et politiques; commentaire article par article* (E. Decaux, Paris, Economica, 2010), at 477. Obs. fin., Fédération de Russie, CCPR/CO79/RUS, 4 November 2003, at para 20.
24. M Bidault, *Article 21 in Le pacte international relatif aux droits civils et politiques; commentaire article par article* (E. Decaux, Paris, Economica, 2010), at 477. Obs. fin., Région administrative spéciale de Hong Kong, CCPR/C/HKG/CO/2, 30 March 2006, at para 20.
25. M Nowak, *UN Covenant on Civil and Political Rights: CCPR Commentary* (Kehl, NP Engel, 2005), at 387; M Bidault, *Article 21 in Le pacte international relatif aux droits civils et politiques;*

commentaire article par article (E. Decaux, Paris, Economica, 2010), at 477–78. *E.g.* Obs. fin. Argentine, CCPR/CO/70/ARG, 1 November 2000, at para 13.
26. Concl. obs., Canada, CCPR/C/CAN/CO/5, at para 20, 28 October 2005. http://www.unhchr.ch/tbs/doc.nsf/(Symbol)/CCPR.C.CAN.CO.5.En
27. *Rassemblement jurassien & Unité jurassienne v Switzerland*, Application No 8191/78. Admissibility decision, 10 October 1979, DR 17, 108, 119.
28. *Oya Ataman v Turkey*, Application No 74552/01. Judgment of 5 December 2006, §16 of the judgment, quoting §29 of the Opinion of the European Commission for Democracy through Law (the Venice Commission) interpreting the OSCE/ODHIR guidelines on drafting laws on freedom of assembly with regard to the regulation of public meetings, adopted at its 64th plenary session (21–22 October 2005).
29. *Oya Ataman v Turkey*, Application No 74552/01. Judgment of 5 December 2006.
30. *Bukta v Hungary*, Application No 25691/04. Judgment of 17 July 2007.
31. See, e.g, *Kivenmaa v Finland*, Comm No 412/1990, 31 March 1994, §9.1.
32. *Chebotareva v Russia*, Comm No 1866/2009, 26 March 2012.
33. *Gryb v Belarus*, Comm No 1316/2004, 26 October 2011.
34. A rather easy HRC case involved the conviction of two persons distributing leaflets organising an "unauthorized mass event" in Belarus does not need to be discussed in detail. See *Zalesskaya v Belarus*, 1604/2007, 28 March 2011. In *Belyazeka v Belarus*, Comm No 1772/2008, 23 March 2012, where a 30-person, peaceful commemoration of Stalinist crimes in a forest was dispersed and the organiser fined for organising an unauthorised mass event, the HRC similarly found a violation of both article 19 and 21.
35. *Chassagnou v France*, Applications Nos 25088/94, 28331/95 and 28443/95. Judgment of 29 April 1999, 1999 ECHR 22, §100.
36. *Tatár & Fáber v Hungary*, Application Nos 26005/08 and 26160/08. Judgment of 12 June 2012.
37. *Rassemblement jurassien & Unité jurassienne v Switzerland*, Application No 8191/78. Admissibility decision of 10 October 1979, DR 17, 108, at 118 *et seq.*, and *Christians Against Racism & Fascism (CARAF) v United Kingdom*, Application No 8440/78. Admissibility decision of 16 July 1980, DR 21, 138, at 148, *Barankevich v Russia*, Application No 10519/03. Judgment of 26 July 2007, §25.
38. *Rassemblement jurassien & Unité jurassienne v Switzerland*, Application No 8191/78. Admissibility decision of 10 October 1979, DR 17, 108, 118 *et seq.*, and *Christians against Racism & Fascism (CARAF) v United Kingdom*, Application No 8440/78. Admissibility decision of 16 July 1980, DR 21, 138, at 148.
39. The Commission noted that "[t]here is ... no indication in the ... case-law that freedom of assembly is intended to guarantee a right to pass and re-pass in public places, or to assemble for purely social purposes anywhere one wishes. Freedom of association, too, has been described as a right for individuals to associate 'in order to attain various ends.'" *Anderson v United Kingdom*, Application No 33689/96. Admissibility decision of 27 October 1997, 25 EHRR CD 172.
40. *E.g. Hashman & Harrup v United Kingdom*, Application No 25594/94. Judgment of 25 November 1999.
41. *E.g. Cox v Louisiana*, 379 U.S. 536 (1965).
42. Explicitly in BVerfG, Beschluß vom 23. 6. 2004 – 1 BvQ 19/04. NJW 2004, 2814. ("Stoppt den Synagogenbau!").
43. *Oberschlick v Austria (No 1)*, Application No 11662/85. Judgment of 23 May 1991, §57.
44. *Women on Waves v Portugal*, Application No 31276/05. Judgment of 3 February 2009, §38–39.
45. *Fáber v Hungary*, Application No 40721/08. Judgment of 24 July 2012, §58.
46. *Fáber v Hungary*, emphasis added.
47. *Tatár & Fáber*, §29.
48. In this case, the fine was imposed with regard to a prior restraint unacceptably on a core political speech, thus the right to freedom of expression, as guaranteed by article 10, was found to have been violated.
49. *Tatár and Fáber*, §40.
50. *Women on Waves v Portugal*, Application No 31276/05. Decision of 3 February 2009.
51. *Coleman v Australia*, Comm No 1157/2003, 17 July 2006.
52. See the strong dissent of Kurt Herndl. M Bidault, *Article 21 in Le pacte international relatif aux droits civils et politiques; commentaire article par article* (E. Decaux, Paris, Economica, 2010), at 480.

53. M Bidault, *Article 21 in Le pacte international relatif aux droits civils et politiques; commentaire article par article* (E. Decaux, Paris, Economica, 2010), at 480.
54. *Chorherr v Austria*, Application No 13308/87. Judgment of 25 August 1993, §31–32.
55. M Rosenfeld, "Constitutional Migration and the Bounds of Comparative Analysis" (2001–2003) 58 NYU Annual Survey of American Law 67–83; or SG Calabresi and KH Rhodes, "The Structural Constitution: Unitary Executive, Plural Judiciary" (1992) 105 Harvard L Rev 1153–1216, at 1199–200.
56. HRC: *Unn & Ben Leirvag v Norway*, Comm No 1155/2003, 23 November 2004; ECtHR: *Folgero v Norway*, Application No 15472/02. Judgment of 29 June 2007.
57. TA El-Haj, "The Neglected Right of Assembly" (2009) 56 UCLA L Rev 543–; JD Inazu, "The Forgotten Freedom of Assembly" (2010) 84 Tulane Law Review 565–612.
58. See, e.g., *Cox v Louisiana*, 379 U.S. 536 (1965), at 555, "emphatically" rejecting that "the First and Fourteenth Amendments afford the same kind of freedom to those who would communicate ideas by conduct such as patrolling, marching, and picketing on streets and highways, as these amendments afford to those who communicate ideas by pure speech."
59. NN, "Reflections on Justice Black and Freedom of Speech" (1972) 6 Val U L Rev 316–331.
60. T Győrfi, "The Importance of Freedom of Assembly: Three Models of Justification", in A Sajó (ed), *Free to Protest: Constituent Power and Street Demonstrations* (Eleven, Utrecht, 2009), 1–17; similarly, D Smilov, "The Power of Assembled People: The Right to Assembly and Political Representation", in A Sajó (ed), *Free to Protest: Constituent Power and Street Demonstrations* (Eleven, Utrecht, 2009), 98–105.
61. G Le Bon, *The Crowd. A Study of the Popular Mind* (MacMillan, New York, 1896); S Freud, *Massenpsychologie und Ich-Analyse* (Internationaler Psychoanalytischer Verlag GmBH, Leipzig, Wien, Zürich, 1921).
62. MR Saleilles, "Conception et objet de la science du droit comparé", in *Congrès international de droit comparé. Procés-verbaux des séances et documents. Tome premier.* (LGDJ, Paris, 1905) 167–189.
63. E Rabel, *Das Recht des Warenkaufs. Eine rechtsvergleichende Darstellung* (2 Bände, Tübingen/Berlin, 1936 and 1957).
64. G Frankenberg, "Critical Comparisons: Re-thinking Comparative Law" (1985) 26 Harvard Int L J 411–456; R Teitel, "Comparative Constitutional Law in a Global Age" (2004) 117 Harvard L Rev 2570–.
65. K Zweigert and H Kötz, *Einführung in die Rechtsvergleichung* (Tübingen, JCB Mohr, 1996).
66. O Kahn-Freund, "On Uses and Misuses of Comparative Law" (1974) 37 Modern Law Review 1–27; I Vörös, "Contextuality and Universality: Constitutional Borrowings on the Global Stage – the Hungarian View" (1998–1999) 1 U of Pennsylvania J of Const L 651–660.
67. A Somek, "The Deadweight of Formulae: What Might Have Been the Second Germanization of American Equal Protection Review" (1998–1999) 1 U of Pennsylvania J of Const L 284–324.
68. R Teitel, "Comparative Constitutional Law in a Global Age" (2004) 117 Harvard L Rev 2570–2697.

Fragmentation in International Human Rights Law: Political Parties and Freedom of Association in the Practice of the UN Human Rights Committee, European Court of Human Rights and Inter-American Court of Human Rights

Svetlana Tyulkina

The article is a part of a Special Issue on institutional fragmentation in international human rights law and it focuses on freedom of association as related to political parties. It investigates how this right is being interpreted and applied in three selected jurisdictions – the UN Human Rights Committee, the European Court of Human Rights and the Inter-American Court of Human Rights. The article starts with analysing the conventional texts regulating the content of the freedom of association and possible limitations states may impose on the exercise of this freedom. It further examines how the freedom of association of political parties is interpreted by three international institutions of human rights protection. Based on an analysis of the conventional texts and the relevant jurisprudence, it investigates whether there is a fragmentation with respect to the freedom of association specific to political parties and what it means for the claim on the universality of human rights.

I. Introduction

In the past decade or so, constitutional and international law scholars and researchers have become increasingly aware and concerned with the phenomenon of fragmentation in international law. Various research studies investigate how to define the fragmentation, what the consequences and implications of substantive and institutional fragmentation are and how much fragmentation international law can accommodate before serious tensions or even conflicts of rules occur between different fields of law and regions of the world.[1]

The introductory piece to this collection of articles holds that the focus of this particular study is institutional fragmentation within a specific field – international human rights law. Contributing authors were asked to narrow their case-studies down to a particular human right and examine the validity of the presumption of normative unity in international human rights law. Each article investigates how similarly or differently selected rights and freedoms are being interpreted and applied by the UN Human Rights Committee, the European Court of Human Rights and the Inter-American Court of Human Rights.

The scope of this article is freedom of association as related to political parties. The freedom of association is, of course, much broader than just freedom to create and join (or not to join) political parties, however it would be too ambitious to attempt to analyse all aspects of this right in one article. The content of this right is very broad and extends to various aspects of social life from sport activities to trade unions. It leads to somewhat different standards of protection accorded to one or another type of association. Also, freedom of association cases often garner consideration for other rights such as freedom of religion for religious associations or freedom of speech or expression for political parties. In this respect it would be difficult to draw a generalised conclusion on how three international human rights mechanisms treat and interpret this right as a whole.

Debates around associational freedom of political parties often overlap with debates on the right to democratic governance (or political participation) and even the more general notion of "democratic society". This can be explained by the fact that founding or joining a political party is one of the tools that citizens can utilise to participate in democratic governance. Furthermore, the freedom to form and join an association, including a political party, belongs to list of rights and freedoms marked out as fundamental to democracy.[2] The amount of scholarly interest in the right to participate in democratic governance in international law and how much popular participation is needed to have fully legitimate and responsible governments is huge.[3] However, having accepted the fact that the freedom of association of political parties may overlay with the right to participate in democratic governance, this article does not aim to address the latter which is indeed a broad and quite independent area of international law. Instead, it focuses on a very narrow dimension of the popular involvement in state affairs, namely, how much freedom political parties enjoy in selected jurisdictions and what techniques and reasoning the judiciary uses to protect them from unfounded attacks by the government and how to prevent political parties harming democracy itself.

The article starts with looking at the conventional texts regulating the content of freedom of association and the possible limitations states may impose on the exercise of this freedom. Further, it will investigate how the freedom of association of political parties is interpreted by three international institutions of human rights protection. By no means did this prove an easy exercise. The European Court of Human Rights has developed an extensive body of case-law on freedom of association in relation to political parties while the two other tribunals have a very modest list of cases on the matter. Also, the spectrum of issues addressed by the three international institutions differs substantially. Based on an analysis of the conventional texts and the relevant jurisprudence, the article will conclude whether there is a fragmentation with respect to the freedom of association specific to political parties and, if so, what the implications are for the claim on the universality of human rights.

II. Freedom of Association Specific to Political Parties: Comparing the Conventions

Texts of international treaties subject to this study provide a certain set of human rights essential to effective political participation, including freedom to form and participate in the activities of political parties. The International Covenant on Civil and Political Rights (ICCPR),[4] the European Convention on Human Rights (ECHR)[5] and the American Convention on Human Rights (ACHR)[6] protect freedom of association in relation to political parties and use quite similar language in their respective provisions. This can be explained by the fact that, with regards to the list of rights, their content and possible limitations, all global and regional human rights treaties are based on and refer to more general provisions of the Universal Declaration of Human Rights.[7]

If we read through the text of the global human rights instrument, ICCPR, article 22 states that everyone shall have the right to freedom of association with others, including the right to form and join trade unions. While the freedom to associate with others in the form of a political party is not directly mentioned in the text of article 22, it is implied given the role of political participation as the very foundation of every democratic state and, furthermore, understanding political parties as key actors in any representative democracy. Additionally, article 22 allows limitations to freedom of association. These limitations must be prescribed by law and be necessary in a democratic society in the interests of national security or public safety, public order (*ordre public*), the protection of public health or morals or the protection of the rights and freedoms of others.

Article 5 of the ICCPR (which is applicable to all rights listed in the Covenant) furthermore addresses the issue of possible limitations imposed on the freedom of association and excludes some political party activities from the protection of the Covenant:

> Nothing in the present Covenant may be interpreted as implying for any State, group or person any right to engage in any activity or perform any act aimed at the destruction of any of the rights and freedoms recognized herein or at their limitation to a greater extent than is provided for in the present Covenant.

This article, as well as its predecessor, article 30 of the Universal Declaration,[8] emerged from past experiences of fascist and other extremist parties gaining power in pre-war Europe through the exercise of protected political rights.[9] It is therefore generally agreed that democracies do not need to wait until a totalitarian-type political party fulfils its program and seizes power; democratic governments can act pre-emptively to prevent a possible political disaster (an idea also known as 'militant democracy', which was introduced into legal scholarship by Karl Loewenstein[10]). Activities of political parties aiming at erosion of human rights and freedoms and damaging democracy are excluded from the protection of the Covenant as well as other human rights instruments included in this study.

Some guarantees of the free formation and functioning of political parties can also be derived from article 25 of the ICCPR, which recognises and protects the right of every citizen to take part in the conduct of public affairs, the right to vote and to be elected, and the right to have access to public service. General Comment No 25 details that the full enjoyment of rights protected by article 25 is dependent on the full enjoyment and respect among others for rights guaranteed in article 22, including freedom to engage in political activity individually or through political parties and other organisations.[11] Further, article 7 of the Convention on the Elimination of All Forms of Discrimination against Women asserts that women should have the right to vote, to stand for election, be involved in the formulation of government policy and actively participate in political parties, lobby groups and NGOs.[12] Provisions of this article were recently put to the test in the Netherlands when the Supreme Court held that that state must take actions to comply with provisions of article 7 in relation to the Reformed Protestant Party (*Staatkuding Gereformeerde Partij*). One of the Party's main views is that women should not be eligible for public office; hence it has no female party members. The matter reached the European Court of Human Rights which found in favour of the national authorities, yet did not provide instruction or guidance to the member states on how exactly to deal with this issue.[13]

Notably, the debate over the limits of freedom of association at the global level is also influenced by the state party's obligation to prohibit and penalise incitement to war and hatred. In this respect, political parties that are allegedly involved in such activities can be limited in their activities or even banned. Thus, the text of article 20 of the ICCPR requires states to prohibit propaganda for war and the advocacy of national, racial, or religious hatred. Article 4(b) of the Convention on Elimination of Racial Discrimination (CERD) details this further:

> States Parties condemn all propaganda and all organizations which are based on ideas or theories of superiority of one race or group of persons of one colour or ethnic origin, or which attempt to justify or promote racial hatred and discrimination in any form, and undertake to adopt immediate and positive measures designed to eradicate all incitement to, or acts of, such discrimination and, to this end, with due regard to the principles embodied in the Universal Declaration of Human Rights and the rights expressly set forth in Article 5 of this Convention, inter alia:
>
> ...
>
> (b) shall declare illegal and prohibit organizations, and also organized and all other propaganda activities, which promote and incite racial discrimination, and shall recognize participation in such organizations or activities as an offence punishable by law.

Altogether, this gives the impression that the UN mechanisms of human rights protection approaches the freedom of association specific to political parties from two somewhat opposite angles. The first stems from provisions of article 22 of the ICCPR which requires states to guarantee the freedom of association (including political parties) and be mindful of a limited list of grounds for restrictions on the right. At the same time, however, article 20 of the ICCPR and article 4 of the CERD call upon states to take actions against associations, including political parties, if they incite racial discrimination. On several occasions, the Committee on the Elimination of Racial Discrimination detected activities which might warrant application of article 20 of the ICCPR and article 4 of the CERD, and expressed concerns even in relation to activities of some political parties' in stable democracies, for example, the UK,[14] Germany[15] and Norway.[16]

Freedom of association in relation to political parties is regulated through fairly similar provisions in the regional human rights instruments – the European and Inter-American Conventions on Human Rights. The central provision of the European Convention on Human Rights is article 11, which guarantees freedom of association and provides the procedure and circumstances under which the right may be limited. In many cases decided by the European Court of Human Rights (ECtHR), relating to the freedom of association of political parties, article 11 was invoked in conjunction with article 10, guaranteeing protection of free speech[17] (this "partnership" is, however, not perfect and some authors have noticed certain incoherence in the case-law concerning these two articles).[18] Further, article 17 of the Convention (the so-called "'abuse clause") places general restrictions on activities aimed at the destruction of any of the rights and freedoms set forth in the Convention in the same fashion as article 30 of the Universal Declaration of Human Rights and article 5 of the ICCPR.

The American Convention on Human Rights guarantees the right to freedom of association in article 16. The article follows the same structural pattern as the other two treaties by first providing the content of the right (to associate freely for ideological, religious, political, economic, labour, social, cultural, sports, or other purposes), and afterwards listing the grounds upon which to impose restrictions on the exercise of the right to associate. Yet, there is a noticeable textual difference between article 16 of the ACHR and the two other treaties; the former provides a more extensive list of potential reasons for citizens wishing to associate, while the latter mentions only trade unions. This, however, does not necessarily mean that the content of the right in practice differs in any substantial way from the two other treaties. In all three jurisdictions, freedom of association was extended to protect citizens exercising this right for reasons listed in article 16 and beyond. Furthermore, acceptable grounds for limiting this right under the IACHR are not different from those present in the ICCPR and the ECHR. This suggests that all three institutions would use the same tests and standards in reviewing state actions imposing restrictions on political parties. This is the subject matter for the following section.

III. Freedom of Association Related to Political Parties: Case-Law Compared

A. Activities excluded from the protection of human rights treaties

Human rights tribunals have had a number of opportunities to express their views on construing the so-called abuse clause.[19] Thus, the Former European Commission of Human Rights has held that article 17 of the Convention was in place "to prevent totalitarian groups from exploiting in their own interest the principles enunciated by the Convention".[20] This statement can be further supported by earlier concerns expressed at the time the Convention was being drafted, namely to prevent by any means "the setting up in one or another of these countries of a regime of the Fascist or Nazi type".[21] The European Court of Human Rights has defined the function of article 17 as "protecting the rights enshrined in the Convention by safeguarding the free functioning of democratic institutions".[22] One of the main objectives of the abuse clause was "to prevent totalitarian or extremist groups from justifying their activities by referring to the Convention"[23] and is closely connected by the court with the notion of self-protective democracy.[24] It was stated that "provisions of the Convention may not be invoked by individuals or their groups for the purpose or intention 'to weaken or destroy the ideals and values of a democratic society'".[25]

The first party closure case to come before the European system was the prohibition of the German Communist Party, declared unconstitutional in accordance with article 21(2) of the German Basic Law.[26] The European Commission of Human Rights did not examine the application in the light of article 10 or 11 of the Convention, rather it applied the abuse clause covered in article 17. In 1979, the Commission decided the case of *Glimmerveen & Hagenbeek v The Netherlands* in a very similar fashion.[27] The applicants were the president and vice-president of a political party prohibited by the Dutch court. The grounds for its prohibition were a Civil Code provision allowing the prohibition of an association if its activities or goals violate public order. As a consequences of this ban, the party lists submitted for the election were later declared invalid, which the applicants claimed was a violation of their right to take part in elections (article 3 of Protocol 1). However, the Commission declared that the applicants could not rely on this article as they intended to use the right guaranteed by this provision for a purpose contrary to the abuse clause of article 17. Since 1998, the ECtHR has dealt with a different type of party prohibition cases and has developed a substantial body of case-law in this field with most of the cases originating from Turkey.

Article 17 has not found widespread support in the court's more recent case-law, at least in relation to political parties. Most likely, the reason for such an approach is the broad and ambiguous language of the provision, introduced into the text of the Convention in the aftermath of the Second World War. The setting in which the Convention was adopted and that in which the court functions are now very different, and may be why the court does not often use this provision. Moreover, once article 17 is invoked, the court has no chance to spell out its opinion on particular issues, thus the majority of such cases are not decided on their merits. The democratisation of Central and Eastern Europe has made the ECtHR reconsider its traditional interpretation in cases concerning the prohibition of political parties supportive of allegedly dangerous ideas and ideologies. Post Central and Eastern European ascension, the court goes beyond merely referring to the abuse clause when striking out such cases.

In a similar fashion, the UN Human Rights Committee held in its 1984 decision *MA v Italy* that reorganising a Fascist party was an act removed from the protection of the Covenant under article 5.[28] It appears that all three international treaties and respective human rights tribunals are familiar with the notion of the so-called "abuse clause" and there were instances when it was applied to deny applicants protection of their right to freedom of association specific to political parties.

B. Freedom of association related to political parties: case-law compared

As revealed above, the three international human rights instruments have almost identical language and structure provisions regulating the limitations states can impose upon individuals exercising their right to associate with others. Does it then follow that political parties enjoy the same level of protection of their freedom of association? Or is there fragmentation in the approach and standards for institutions when deciding on whether a state party has violated an applicant's freedom of association by restricting activities or banning a party?

Freedom of association in relation to political parties in the jurisprudence of the UN Human Rights Committee

Without a doubt, the ECtHR jurisprudence covers the issue of prohibition of political parties in much more detail than its two counterparts analysed in this study. This is, however, due to the fact that several cases on political party limitation have reached the court in last couple of decades, and the court has had ample opportunity to interpret the Convention's norms in relation to political parties. In its interpretation, the ECtHR sent a strong message to all member states that protection of political parties is taken very seriously by the Convention's bodies. Moreover, member states are expected to grant substantial protection even to unpopular political groups. The two other human rights institutions have not yet been given such a chance. Therefore looking for detailed tests and standards of interpreting freedom of association specific to political parties might appear less rewarding.

Generally, the level of attention given by the ICCPR and the Human Rights Committee to freedom of association, especially in relation to political parties, is rather disappointing to say the least. For example, article 22, which guarantees freedom of association, is not the subject matter of a General Comment as is the case for most of other rights provisions in the Covenant. Nor is it discussed in great detail in any of the existing General Comments. For instance, details on the guarantees of activities of political parties could have been covered in General Comment on article 25 (the right to participate in the conduct of public affairs and the right to vote). However, as was revealed above, while General Comment No 25 does mention political parties, it does so very briefly. A study on obligations relevant to democratic governance suggests that freedom of association specific to political parties needs further attention and clarification by the ICCPR bodies.[29] For example, the study concludes that key aspects of party registration are only implicitly regulated. This includes requirements for registration of rules and a prohibition on excessively restrictive registration procedures. Human Rights Committee (HRC) decisions have developed criteria for party registration only in general terms. With regards to the banning of political parties, the HRC sets only general and vague requirements and the major test applicable is proportionality. A new General Comment could be a very valuable addition to the interpretation of article 22 and potentially clarify some of these urgent matters.

Also, as mentioned above, political parties are not explicitly mentioned in the text of the Covenant, an aspect that has its own specific reasons. The ICCPR drafting process was significantly affected by the Cold War tensions. Given the time in which the drafting process took place, it is not surprising that the drafters of this global treaty could not reach a compromise over the political parties issue.[30] While western states have had a long-standing commitment to the multi-party system, many socialist states did not consider it as a prerequisite for true democracy. Some even saw multiple political parties as a possible cause of civil war and violence in non-homogenous societies.[31] Hence, any direct reference to the multi-party system would result in a substantial number of states turning away from the initiative and thus not signing the treaty.

The first instance in which the HRC had to deal with the freedom of association specific to political parties was a submission from an Italian citizen, MA, who was convicted of involvement in reorganising a dissolved fascist party.[32] The Committee concluded that any attempt to reorganise a party of such a nature fell outside of the protection of the Covenant (under article 5). Consequently, the communication was declared inadmissible. In 2002, the HRC delivered its decision on the case of *Arenz v Germany*.[33] The communication concerned three German citizens who were members of the Church of Scientology and members of the Christian Democratic Union (CDU), one of the two major political parties in Germany. In 1991, the CDU National Convention adopted a resolution declaring affiliation with the Church of Scientology as incompatible with CDU membership.[34] The applicants claimed that their expulsion from the CDU violated, inter alia, article 22. In separate proceedings, German national courts dismissed all legal actions based on principles of party autonomy and obligations to an internal democratic organisation (under article 21 of the German Basic Law).[35] According to the German judiciary, political party obligations to an internal democratic organisation prevailed over the applicants' rights to freedom of expression, association and religion. This rights dispute was to be the main issue before the Committee. However, the Committee held that it was not a fourth instance appellate body. Unless proceedings before the domestic courts were arbitrary, the Committee is not competent to re-evaluate findings of facts or re-evaluate the application of domestic legislation.[36] As such, the HRC left unanswered its views on issues of internal party democracy imposed by domestic legislation and how far state parties could go to affect individuals' right to freedom of association. This communication was dropped at the point where it was about to become a valuable contribution to the debate.

The freedom to form and participate in the activities of political parties is a more salient element of the freedom of association specific to political parties. However, there are instances when international human rights institutions were asked to rule on the requirement of political participation exclusively through political parties. In other words, some states indirectly "force" individuals to associate with others in the form of political parties in order to be elected to the state's legislative bodies. The HRC has recently handed down a decision on a communication brought by a citizen of Russia.[37] Among the alleged violations claimed by the applicant was one under article 25. The applicant claimed that he could not take part in federal elections, as Russia's electoral system does not allow the standing of independent candidates in elections to the Federal Parliament. The communication was brought and examined mainly under article 25 (not article 22). In the end, the HRC dismissed the communication, concluding that the claim was insufficiently substantiated. Thus the outcome provides no clarity to the question concerning the use of coercion to join political parties to stand for elections. The outcome can also be seen as a missed opportunity to address concerns about current political situation in Russia. As the Committee correctly pointed out, an individual can join a political party to sign up for federal elections, however it is not realistic to expect any political party to allow this. What is even less likely is the creation of a new political party under that existing in the 2008 legislative regime.[38] In the light of the ECtHR decision *Republican Party of Russia v Russia*[39] and the Venice Commission Opinion on electoral law of Russia,[40] the HRC's question of why the author could not create his own political party together with individuals sharing similar political opinions and stand for elections through it, sounds slightly sarcastic.

The case-law of the HRC does not provide any further detailed insight to the issue of freedom of association specific to political parties (or in relation to freedom of association in general, with only 8 cases decided under article 22 of the Covenant).[41] Both the HRC's unwillingness to go into detail in the above-mentioned cases and its general approach towards the associational freedom of political parties in comparison with the ECtHR (ie the General Comment on the right to freedom of association or any other similar soft-law instrument) is most likely to explain the different role and functions of these human rights instruments. While the ICCPR is a global treaty and aims to monitor the human rights situation around the world, the ECHR is a regional instrument. Furthermore, the Council of Europe consists of member states that share a rather similar political and social background as well as strong traditions of a commitment to democracy with multiple political parties playing a major role in the process of democratic decision-making.

Political parties and jurisprudence of the European Court of Human Rights

A case-study of the ECtHR reveals that providing an analysis of the court's practice in relation to freedom of association of political parties is a rewarding but complex exercise. This institution has produced a comprehensive and extensive body of case-law in this field, including prohibition and other limitations that state parties may impose on political parties. At the very beginning, the court and former Commission had to deal mainly with cases concerning the supporters of fascist or communist ideologies. In regards to these actors, the court developed a fairly consistent and rather simple line of argument. Most such applications were declared either manifestly ill-founded or struck down under article 17 of the Convention (the so-called abuse clause discussed above).[42]

The first case on party prohibition decided on its merits by the ECtHR following the *Glimmerveen & Hagenbeek* case (mentioned above), was the case of *United Communist Party v Turkey*.[43] This case is one of the most far-reaching decisions in the court's jurisprudence on permissible limitations imposed on political parties. The ECtHR refers to this decision and cites the main findings and principles established in this judgment in nearly all cases on party prohibition decided thereafter.

The Principal State Counsel at the court of Cassation that brought proceedings in the Turkish Constitutional Court argued that the United Communist Party of Turkey (TBKP) sought to establish the domination of one social class over the others.[44] The TBKP were accused of having incorporated the word "communist" into its name;[45] having carried out activities likely to undermine the territorial integrity of the state and the unity of the nation;[46] and declaring itself successor to a previously dissolved political party, the Turkish Workers' Party.[47] The Constitutional Court rejected some of the alleged violations but nevertheless held that the mere fact that a political party included in its name a word prohibited by section 96(3) of the Law on Political Parties no 2820 ("communist"), sufficed to trigger the application of the provision. Consequently, the party was dissolved, incurring all the consequences prescribed by the Constitution.[48]

The Party leadership lodged a complaint with the ECtHR, which found a violation of article 11 of the Convention.[49] As there were more applications from Turkey awaiting hearing at the ECtHR, the court seized its chance to send a message to all member states to guide them in the practice of imposing limitations on activities of political parties. First of all, the court explicitly extended protection of article 11 to political parties, stating that political parties are a form of association essential to the proper functioning of democracy.[50] Secondly, the court stated that a "political party cannot be not excluded from the protection afforded by the Convention simply because its activities are regarded by the national authorities as undermining the constitutional structures of the State and calling for the imposition of restrictions".[51] Thirdly, all political and institutional organisations of member states must accordingly respect the rights and principles enshrined in the Convention: "It matters little in this context whether the provisions in issue are constitutional or merely legislative".[52] The court made clear that it does not discern any difference between constitutional and legislative provisions when exercising its jurisdictions. Nothing from a member state's jurisdiction is excluded from scrutiny under the Convention.

In its further arguments, the court reiterated that the Convention is intended to guarantee rights that are not theoretical or illusory but practical and effective, which would not be the case if article 11 were limited to only the founding of an association. In addition, the court drew attention to the precedent that "Article 11 must also be considered in the light of Article 10 as protection of opinions and the freedom to express them is one of the objectives of the freedoms of assembly and association as enshrined in Article 11".[53] As the court has said many times before, in relation to article 10, there can be no democracy without pluralism. Freedom of expression as enshrined in article 10 is applicable to political parties that support or promote ideas that offend, shock or disturb, and the state is the ultimate guarantor of this principle.[54] At the same time, the court admitted that a state's institutions could not be deprived of the right to protect those institutions and "some compromise between the requirements of defending democratic society and individual rights is inherent in the system of the Convention".[55] Further, the court clarified that the exceptions set out in articles 10 and 11 shall be construed strictly where political parties are concerned. Only convincing and compelling reasons can justify restrictions on freedom of association imposed on political parties.

Applying these principles, the court found it necessary to examine the party's constitution and program to investigate its true objectives and its leaders' intentions. As to the party's name, the court ruled that a political party's name in general is not enough to justify its dissolution. Furthermore, in relation to TBKP's political goals, the court declared:

> The court considers one of the principal characteristics of democracy to be the possibility it offers of resolving a country's problems through dialogue, without recourse to violence, even when they are irksome. Democracy thrives on freedom of expression. From that point of view, there can be no justification for hindering a political group solely because it seeks to debate in public the situation of part of the State's population and to take part in the nation's political life in order to find, according to democratic rules, solutions capable of satisfying everyone concerned.[56]

Therefore, the court concluded that measures as drastic as the immediate and permanent dissolution of the TBKP, ordered before its activities had even begun and coupled with a ban barring its leaders from discharging any other political responsibility, is disproportionate to the aim pursued and consequently unnecessary in a democratic society (in violation of article 11).

Only four months later, the ECHR issued a judgment on the case of *Socialist Party of Turkey v Turkey*.[57] The court mainly reaffirmed its previous judgment and stated that "the fact that the party's political program is considered incompatible with the current principles and structures of the Turkish State does not make it incompatible with the rules of democracy".[58] This case was followed by a few other cases from Turkey concerning mainly Kurdish parties and, in all of them, Turkey was found in violation of the Convention.[59] This case is notable for the reason that the party dissolved itself before the Constitutional Court decided on the case. However, this move did not help the party to avoid a declaration of dissolution by the Constitutional Court with all the prescribed consequences.

Principles proclaimed in the *TBKP* case and subsequent cases indicate that political parties enjoy a broad protection of their freedom of association. It does not matter that a party proposes changes and ideas incompatible with the national constitution. The most pressing problems of the state should be actively debated through open dialogue. In line with this statement was the *Zhechev v Bulgaria* judgment, concerning the dissolution of, not a political party, but a public association. The ECtHR held that even where an association was trying to achieve goals contrary to the Constitution, an interference (or rather, dissolution) is not necessarily justified. Therefore, the court appears to give a wide protection to political parties and all other actors involved in coining public opinion in political matters.

This conclusion, however, might be challenged in the light of the *Refah Partisi v Turkey* decision in 2001.[60] For the first time, the ECtHR supported the decision of the Turkish government to dissolve a political party. The court also took this opportunity to systemise its views on how a political party may campaign for a change in the law or the legal and constitutional basis of the state: (a) the means used to that end must in every respect be legal and democratic; and (b) the change proposed must itself be compatible with fundamental democratic principles.[61]

While these principles are completely consistent with the court's previous jurisprudence, the way in which they were applied in *Refah Partisi* case is somewhat problematic and alarming. It appears as though the court struggles when adjudicating cases that go beyond the traditional paradigm in which minor political parties are "bullied" by their dominating counterparts. In such instances, the court engages in a detailed analysis of its decision, including a provocative and somewhat aggressive statement that Islam and democracy are incompatible, implying that the presence of the former in politics excludes any possibility of coexisting with democracy. But nevertheless, it is important to acknowledge that this judgment is an important contribution to the field. For example, it restated that states have a very narrow margin of appreciation when it comes to the prohibition of political parties yet, at the same time, they are not required to wait until a political party has seized power and taken concrete steps to implement a policy incompatible with the standards of the Convention and democracy.[62] These findings were employed by the court in other subsequent cases on prohibition of political parties.[63]

However, the freedom of association of political parties is not only limited to cases involving states in order to dissolve political party. The ECtHR dealt with other possible limitations such as mandatory registration procedures, temporary suspension of party activities, exclusion from a state's financial supervision, electoral threshold, etc. As to registration procedures, it was interpreted by ECtHR bodies that the requirement of registration for political parties, *per se*, is not a violation of the Convention.[64] However, contracting parties do not have unlimited discretion to choose which, and how serious, the requirements imposed on parties wishing to register should be.

The ECtHR uses the same standards in cases of party bans and denial of registration: refusal of registration must be possible in a democratic society if it meets the proportionality test.[65] A refusal to register a party can be applied only in extreme cases where there is evidence that the party has not sought to pursue its aims by lawful and democratic means, or when a party proposes changes to the law which are incompatible with fundamental democratic principles.[66] The court has not always been supportive of political parties that are denied state registration. In the admissibility decision of *Artymov v Russian Federation*, the ECtHR found in favour of national authorities whose practice to deny registration was based on the legislative provision prohibiting organising political parties along religious or ethnic affiliation.[67]

While the issue of a temporary ban or closure of political parties has not arisen often, the ECtHR takes this measure as a serious constraint on party activities, noting that it may have a "chilling effect" on a party's freedom. The case of *Christian Democratic People's Party v Moldova* demonstrates such an approach.[68] Here, the temporary closure of the party was sought in response to allegedly unauthorised demonstrations organised against various governmental proposals. Pointedly, the closure was imposed on the eve of the parliamentary elections. This, combined with the communist affiliation of the then ruling party in Moldova, likely triggered the extremely negative reaction of the Strasbourg court, which stated that only very serious breaches could justify a ban on the activities of a political party (such as endangering fundamental democratic principles, or political pluralism).

The Council of Europe's soft law on the freedom of association specific to political parties

In 1998, in response to the growing number of cases before the Strasbourg court regarding limitations imposed on political parties, the Secretary General of the Council of Europe requested the European Commission for Democracy through Law (Venice Commission) to conduct a survey on the prohibition of political parties and analogous measures. The concern expressed by the Council of Europe was not only limited to cases originating from Turkey, but was also spurred on by the fact that most of the post-communist European states included in their legislation and constitutions a possibility of sanctioning the behaviour of political parties. The Venice Commission conducted research to study the situation existing in different member states and later adopted the *Guidelines on Prohibition and Dissolution of Political Parties and Analogous Measures*.[69] This document consists of seven major points and it echoes the ECHR jurisprudence on matters such as the importance of political parties for a stable democratic system and the wide protection accorded to political parties in order to prevent government from unjustified intrusion into party activities. Thus, section 3 of the document allows "for dissolution of political parties only in cases where parties advocate for the use of violence or use it as a political means to overthrow the democratic constitutional order but allows advocating for peaceful change of the Constitution".[70]

The three-prong salient recommendation for the member states is that (i) prohibition of political parties should be treated only as a measure of last resort; (ii) parties facing dissolution proceedings must be given strong judicial protection; and (iii) decisions on dissolution should be made by a constitutional court or other appropriate judicial body. The Council of Europe is still committed to promoting the same principles as established in

1999. For example, in 2008 the Venice Commission "was asked to review the constitutional and legal provisions which are relevant to the prohibition of political parties in Turkey".[71] The Commission found that the 1998 report still represents a concise summary of European practice, reiterating and confirming its conclusions.[72]

To conclude, there is a clear, common European approach to the issue of how a democracy should respond to attempts which threaten it by opening a free marketplace of ideas, capable of neutralising extremist and allegedly dangerous ideologies, and allowing ideas of democracy to flourish. The ECtHR has a developed body of case-law that in general supports the possibility of preventive action being taken by democratic states in order to prevent harm to the established order, including the possibility of banning/dissolving political parties. However, states are only allowed to utilise such radical and drastic measures in extreme situations.

Freedom of association and political parties in the jurisprudence of the Inter-American Court of Human Rights

Experience of the Inter-American Court of Human Rights (IACHR) dealing with freedom of association in relation to political parties is far from being close to that of the European court. Case-law of the IACHR does not provide a significant insight on how broad or narrow the protection of political parties under the Convention is. However, before placing blame on the court for this, some important observations are in order.

Throughout its entire history, the Organisation of American States[73] had to struggle with tension between the protection of democracy at the regional level and respecting the principle of non-intervention in national affairs.[74] It was only in 1991 that this organisation took the first serious step in favour of the protection of democracy over the principle of non-intervention by adopting the Santiago Commitment to Democracy[75] and Resolution 1080 on Representative Democracy.[76] Protecting human rights and the principle of non-intervention are not easily reconciled, and it took enormous efforts for the inter-American human rights system to make its member states acknowledge that human rights and their protection are not entirely internal matters (157).

Furthermore, since its very first days, this regional human rights court has been busy with grave human rights violations such as forced disappearances and arbitrary killings linked to government actions, often occurring during periods of military control. Also, the court has never experienced large number of complaints or requests for advisory opinions. During its first fifteen years, for instance, the Inter-American Court delivered five decisions on the merits and issued fourteen advisory opinions.[77] Given this situation, it appears that the court simply did not have an opportunity to interpret and apply article 16 of the Convention in general, and in relation to political parties in particular. In this respect, the level of protection granted to political parties by the Convention is not as clear and precise as in Europe. This notwithstanding, political associations in the region are regarded as important components to successful and stable democratic regimes.

In general, the court recognises the importance of freedom of association and notes that "the rights to freedom of … association have been broadly recognized as significant individual civil as well as political rights that protect against arbitrary interference by the state when persons choose to associate with others, and are fundamental to the existence and functioning of a democratic society".[78] Further, the same document details that "the protection of such rights may entail not only the obligation of a state not to interfere with the exercise of the right of … association, but in certain circumstances may require positive measures on the part of the state to secure the effective exercise of the freedom ..."[79] Similarly to the ECHR and ICCPR, the rights to freedom of association in the American Convention are not designed as non-derogable and any measures taken by states to suspend these rights must comply strictly with the rules and principles governing derogation, including the principles of necessity and proportionality.

Furthermore, political parties are seen as playing an essential role in promoting the equality of women's political participation, which is a rather sore issue for the region.[80] The Inter-American Commission recognises that a number of countries in the region make serious efforts to promote the political participation of women. It is therefore legitimately expected that the freedom of association specific to political parties is fully supported by the Convention's bodies to promote democracy and popular participation in conducting state affairs. However, no soft-law instruments provide any sort of detailed guidance on the treatment of political parties as an aspect of the exercise of the right to freedom of association. Nor does the case-law of the IACHR offer sufficient guidance to member states on how limitations on the freedom of association should operate in practice, yet also preventing any rise in the activities of potentially dangerous political parties.

As to the jurisprudence of the IACHR, it indicated on a few occasions that article 16(1) establishes that anyone who is subject to the jurisdiction of a state party has the right to associate freely with others, without any intervention by the public authorities that restricts or obstructs the exercise of this right.[81] In addition, the court has observed that freedom of association also "gives rise to positive obligations to prevent attacks against it, to protect those who exercise it, and to investigate violations of this freedom".[82] These positive obligations must be adopted, according to the court, even in the sphere of relations between individuals, when necessary.[83]

One of the central cases related to political parties in IACHR jurisprudence would be *Yatama v Nicaragua*.[84] Yatama (which means "Organisation of the sons of Mother Earth") is considered protector and representative of the ingenious communities of Nicaragua. As of 1990, it began to take part in regional elections, but as a public association rather than a political party. In 2000, a law was adopted which limited participation in the elections to registered political parties. The Supreme Electoral Council excluded Yatama from the 2000 elections as it allegedly had not obtained legal status as a political party. This decision had a considerable impact on the outcome of the elections, in which a large number of the indigenous population abstained from voting, feeling they were not represented in the elections. While the case is of a rather technical nature, and was not decided under article 16, it nevertheless sends a strong message: political parties are considered major instruments to ensure popular participation in governance and public affairs, especially in relation to indigenous political groups. This case is considered a landmark legal precedent, guaranteeing indigenous peoples right to political participation.[85] For the purpose of this study, this case also provides that positive obligations imposed on states in relation to political parties and other political associations should be taken very seriously. The jurisprudence of the IACHR specific to political parties is not as comprehensive as that of the ECHR, yet it provides interesting insight on how political parties are being treated in a region where many states do not have stable democratic traditions and are still on their way to establishing meaningful democratic regimes.

Another instructive insight to the issue of freedom of association specific to political parties comes from the case of *Castaneda Gutman v Mexico*.[86] The circumstances of this case are similar to *AP v Russia* discussed earlier in the section on the UN Human Rights Committee. The applicant, Castaneda Gutman, was refused registration as an independent candidate for the 2006 presidential elections as electoral law states that only national political parties can register candidates for elected office. Just as in *AP*, there were other opportunities to participate in elections such as joining a political party or creating a national political group that would indicate a formal agreement to participate with a political party.[87] The court concluded that the system of election was in accordance with the national constitution and did not contravene the norms of the American Convention. In this respect, we can observe that two human rights institutions abstained from dictating to states the desired electoral system and are satisfied with the presence of other options available for independent candidates.

IV. Concluding Remarks

This study on comparing the freedom of association for political parties has revealed that all three human rights instruments guarantee and extend this right to political parties in their jurisdictions. Political parties are recognised in all jurisdictions as key players in representative democracy and they facilitate the process of popular participation in conducting state affairs. Moreover, the multi-party system is considered desirable and the only one compatible with the major principles of democracy in all human rights regimes.

Freedom to form a political party and participate in its activities is not considered to be non-derogable right. All three treaties provide a list of grounds for imposing limitations on the exercise of such a right. That these grounds are nearly identical textually indicates that there is little disagreement regarding how and when states can put restrictions on the activities of political parties. All three treaties concerned do not treat the idea to ban political parties (permanently or temporarily) from the political processes as an unconditional violation of the right to freedom of association. As grounds for the imposition of limitations to freedom of association do not differ, the ECHR, the HRC and the ICCPR rely on the same standards and tests when limiting or suspending activities of political parties. Such restrictions will have to pass the necessity test that involves the assessment of whether there is a need to introduce such restrictions, and whether they are proportionate to the aim pursued.

These findings lead to the conclusion that there are no grounds to declare the presence of substantive *normative* divergences or convergences. This is due to the fact that all treaties are based on the principles established and proclaimed by the Universal Declaration of Human Rights. The normative convergence is further supported by the rather universal agreement that political parties and their activities are essential elements of democracy and it is in the best interest of any true democracy to encourage their active involvement in dialogue between government and citizen. However, it is false to claim that the protection of political parties across the three jurisdictions is void of any elements of substantive divergence.

The major substantial difference is the precision with which the three international human rights instrument treat the freedom of association specific to political parties and which aspects of this right receive attention from human rights institutions. The Council of Europe and the European Court of Human Rights developed a comprehensive legal (including soft-law measures) and judicial mechanism in relation to limitations imposed on political parties. The ECtHR seized the opportunity and indeed played the role of policy-maker when it gave a very detailed account of how states should act when banning a political party. While the HRC and the IACHR do not have such an impressive record of cases on the freedom of association specific to political parties, and look at political parties from a different angle, this situation may be improved upon by adopting soft-law instruments (akin to the guidance produced by the Venice Commission), or allowing cases to advance to the merits stage rather than striking them down for procedural violations.

Another noticeable difference is that the UN mechanism is very concerned with imposing obligations on states to ban organisations with allegedly racist agendas, whereas the inter-American mechanism greatly focuses on imposing positive obligations on the state to ensure that the right to associate is not an illusory one. Similar references can be found in the text of the ECHR and the ECtHR case-law. For example the prohibition of political party Batasuna in Spain was seen by some as compatible with the positive obligations of member states,[88] the latter nevertheless strongly focuses on the exceptionality of such a measure.

Do these observations on freedom of association specific to political parties indicate some degree of fragmentation of international human rights law, and as a result, challenge the notion of the universality of human rights? The answer is more yes than no. However, it does not necessarily have a negative connotation. Each international, be it global or regional, human rights system is unique and has its own purpose, a reflection of distinct political authority and legal powers. Furthermore, political, social, legal, cultural, historical circumstances vary from one region to another. It is therefore not easy to find a universal approach or solution to accommodate all these differences. In this respect, fragmentation in international human rights is inevitable. At the same time, it should not be treated as something negative or harmful. Fragmentation has its place in international human rights to allow each system to preserve its autonomy and uniqueness, and to adjust to local conditions in which these instructions function. Taken as a whole, fragmentation decreases tensions surrounding the accusation that western values and the hegemony of the European Human Rights project have been imposed on the rest of the world. There are few possibilities that all human rights institutions will become exact copies of the European Court of Human Rights model and there is nothing wrong with that. There is institutional and substantive fragmentation in international human rights law and it is in place to facilitate dialogue and cooperation between systems whilst also preserving the autonomy of each human rights system at the global and regional level. Be that as it may, it is also important to encourage international human rights institutions to learn and perhaps borrow successful legal and judicial techniques and approaches from other jurisdictions.

Notes

1. For example: P-M Dupuy, "A Doctrinal Debate in the Globalisation Era: On the 'Fragmentation' of International Law" (2007) 1 European J of Legal Studies 1–19; M Koskenniemi and P Leino, "Fragmentation of International Law? Postmodern Anxieties" (2006) 15 Leiden J of Int Law 553–79; M Koskenniemi, *Report on Fragmentation of International Law: Difficulties Arising from the Diversification and Expansion of International Law* (, 2006); MA Young, *Regime Interaction in International Law: Facing Fragmentation* (Cambridge UP, Cambridge, 2011); International Law Commission, *Conclusions of the Work of the Study Group on the Fragmentation of International Law: Difficulties Arising from the Diversification and Expansion of International Law* (Yearbook of the International Law Commission, 2006).
2. For a more detailed account of this statement in relation to the European Convention on Human Rights see, for example, S Marks, "The European Convention on Human Rights and its 'Democratic Society'", *British Yearbook of International Law* (1996) 209–38; H-M Napel, "The European Court of Human Rights and Political Rights: The Need for More Guidance" (2009) 5 European Const Law Rev 464–80.
3. See, for example, S Marks, "The European Convention on Human Rights and its 'Democratic Society'", *British Yearbook of International Law* (1996) 209–38; S Marks, "The 'Emerging Norm': Conceptualizing 'Democratic Governance'" (1997) 91 American Soc of Int Law 372–76; S Marks, "What has Become of the Emerging Right to Democratic Governance?" (2011) 22(2) Int J of Int

Law 507–24; GH Fox and BR Roth (eds), *Democratic Governance and International Law* (Cambridge UP, Cambridge, 2000); J D'Aspermont, "The Rise and Fall of Democratic Governance in International Law: a Reply to Susan Marks" (2011) 22(2) European J of Int Law 549–70; S Wheatley, *The Democratic Legitimacy of International Law* (Hart Publishing, Oxford, 2010), at 92–246, 311–33, and some others.

4. International Covenant on Civil and Political Rights, adopted and opened for signature, ratification and accession by the General Assembly Resolution 2200A (XXI) of 16 December 1966. Entered into force: 23 March 1976. State Parties as of November 2013: 167.
5. Convention for the Protection of Human Rights and Fundamental Freedoms, CETS 005, opened for signature on 4 November 1950. Entered into force: 3 September 1953. State Parties: 47.
6. American Convention of Human Rights. Adopted 22 November 1969. Entered into force: 18 July 1978. State Parties as of November 2013: 23.
7. Universal Declaration of Human Rights. Adopted and proclaimed by General Assembly Resolution 217A (III) of 10 December 1948.
8. Article 30: Nothing in this Declaration may be interpreted as implying for any State, group or person any right to engage in any activity or to perform any act aimed at the destruction of any of the rights and freedoms set forth herein.
9. More details are provided in, for example, in GH Fox and G Nolte, "Intolerant Democracies" (1995) 36 Harvard Law Rev 1–70, at 40.
10. See K Loewenstein, "Militant Democracy and Fundamental Rights I, II" (1937) 3 American Pol Sci Rev 417–432; and (1937) 3 American Pol Sci Rev 4: 638–58.
11. General Comment No 25: The Right to Participate in Public Affairs, Voting Rights and the Right of Equal Access to Public Service (article 25). Adopted 12 July 1996 at the Fifty-seventh Session of the Human Rights Committee.
12. The Convention on the Elimination of All Forms of Discrimination against Women. Adopted by the UN General Assembly 18 December 1979. Entered into force: 3 September 1981. State Parties as of November 2013: 187.
13. *Staatkuding Gereformeerde Partij v The Netherlands*, Application 58369/10. Judgment of 10 July 2012.
14. United Kingdom of Great Britain and Northern Ireland, CERD, A/48/18 (1993) 73, at paras 416 and 421.
15. Germany, CERD, A/48/18 (1993) 81, at paras 446 and 449.
16. Norway, CERD, A/52/18 (1997) 77, at paras 606 and 607.
17. Article 10: 1. Everyone has the right to freedom of expression. this right shall include freedom to hold opinions and to receive and impart information and ideas without interference by public authority and regardless of frontiers. This article shall not prevent States from requiring the licensing of broadcasting, television or cinema enterprises.
18. See S Sottiaux and S Rummens "Concentric Democracy: Resolving the Incoherence in the European Court of Human Rights' Case Law on Freedom of Expression and Freedom of Association" (2012) 10(1) Int J of Const Law 106–26.
19. GH Fox and G Nolte, "Intolerant Democracies" (1995) 36 Harvard Law Rev 1–70, at 41.
20. *Lawless v Ireland*, Application 332/57, Decision of the Former European Commission of Human Rights of 1 July 1961; *De Becker v Belgium*, Application 214/56, Decision of the Former European Commission of Human Rights of 23 March 1962, at para 137: article 17 of the European Convention "applies only to persons who threaten the democratic system of the Contracting Parties".
21. S Marks, "The European Convention on Human Rights and its 'Democratic Society'", *British Yearbook of International Law* (1996) 209–38, at 210.
22. *KPD v Federal Republic of Germany*, Application 250/57. Decision of the Former European Commission of Human Rights of 20 July 1957.
23. *Zdanoka v Latvia*, Application 58278/00. Judgment of 16 March 2006.
24. DJ Harris, M O'Boyle, E Bates and C Buckley, *Law of the European Convention on Human Rights* (Oxford UP, Oxford, 2009), at 649.
25. DJ Harris, M O'Boyle, E Bates and C Buckley, *Law of the European Convention on Human Rights* (Oxford UP, Oxford, 2009).
26. *KPD v Federal Republic of Germany*.

27. *Limmerveen & Hagenbeek v The Netherlands*, Applications 8348/78, 8406/78. Decision of the Former European Commission of Human Rights of 11 October 1979.
28. *MA v Italy* (117/1981), ICCPR, A/39/40 (10 April 1984) at para 190.
29. The Carter Center: Democracy Reporting Internationally, *Overview of State Obligations Relevant to Democratic Governance and Democratic Elections*. Policy Paper. Available at http://www.democracy-reporting.org/publications/thematic-papers.html.
30. GH Fox, "The Right to Political Participation in International Law" in GH Fox and BR Roth (eds), *Democratic Governance and International Law* (Cambridge UP, Cambridge, 2000), 48–90, at 55.
31. GH Fox, "The Right to Political Participation in International Law" in GH Fox and BR Roth (eds), *Democratic Governance and International Law* (Cambridge UP, Cambridge, 2000), 48–90, at 56.
32. *MA v. Italy*, (117/1981), ICCPR, A/39/40 (10 April 1984) 190.
33. *Arenz v Germany* (1138/2002), A/59/40 vol. II (24 March 2004) 548.
34. *Arenz v Germany*, at para 2.2.
35. *Arenz v Germany*, at paras 3.1, 3.2, 3.3 and 3.4.
36. *Arenz v Germany*, at para 8.6.
37. *AP v Russian Federation*, Communication No 1857/2008, 28 March 2013.
38. The Communication was submitted in 2008. The status and activities of political parties were governed by the Political Parties Act Federal Law No 95 – FZ of 11 July 2001. Section 3 §2 required that a political party should have no fewer than 50,000 members and should have regional branches with no fewer than 500 members in more than one half of Russia's regions. Law No 95 was substantially changed in this aspect in 2012 when the requirement for the minimum number of party members was cut to 500.
39. *Republican Party of Russia v Russia*, Application 12976/07. Judgment of 12 April 2011, para 58.
40. Opinion of the European Commission to Democracy through Law on the Federal Law on the Election of the Deputies of the State Duma of the Russian Federation. Adopted by the Council for Democratic Elections on 15 March 2012 and by the Venice Commission on 16–17 May 2012.
41. *Wallman v Austria*, Communication No 1002/2001, 1 April 2004; *Lee v Republic of Korea*, Communication No 1119/2002, 20 July 2005; *Zvozskov v Belarus*, Communication No 1039/2001, 17 October 2006; *Korneenko v Belarus*, Communication No 1274/2004, 31 October 2006; *Belyatsky v Belarus*, 1296/2004, 24 July 2007; *Katsora v Belarus*, 1 Communication No 383/2005, 25 October 2010; *Kungurov v Uzbekistan*, Communication No 1478/2006, 20 July 2011; *Korneenko v Belarus*, Communication No 1226/2003, 20 July 2012.
42. P Harvey, "Militant Democracy and the European Convention on Human Rights" (2004) 29(3) European Law Rev 407–20.
43. General comments on this case are provided by DJ Harris, M O'Boyle, E Bates and C Buckley, *Law of the European Convention on Human Rights* (Oxford UP, Oxford, 2009), at 527–28; RCA White and C Ovey, *The European Convention on Human Rights* (Oxford UP, Oxford, 2010), at 463–65; and P Dijk, F van Hoof, A van Rijn and L Zwaak, *Theory and Practice of the European Convention of Human Rights* (Intersentia, 2006).
44. These actions are prohibited by articles 6, 10 and 14 and former article 68 of the Constitution of Turkey, and section 78 of the Law on Political Parties No 2820 (adopted in 1983).
45. This appears to be contrary to section 96(3) of Law on Political Parties No 2820.
46. These activities are prohibited by articles 2, 3 and 66 and former article 68 of the Constitution, and sections 78 and 81 of Law on Political Parties No 2820.
47. This is prohibited activity under section 96(2) of Law No 2820.
48. According to article 69(9) of the Turkish Constitution, a party which has been dissolved permanently cannot be founded under another name. Article 69(10) establishes that "Members, including the founders, of a political party whose acts or statements have caused the party to be dissolved permanently cannot be founders, members, directors or supervisors in any other party for a period of five years from the date of publication in the official gazette of the Constitutional Court's final decision and its justification for permanently dissolving the party."
49. *United Communist Party of Turkey v Turkey*, Application 133/1996/752/951. Judgment of 30 January 1998.
50. *United Communist Party of Turkey v Turkey*.
51. *United Communist Party of Turkey v Turkey*.

52. *United Communist Party of Turkey v Turkey*, at para 30.
53. *United Communist Party of Turkey v Turkey*, at para 52.
54. First stated by the court in *Handyside v United Kingdom*, Application 5493/72. Judgment of 7 December 1976.
55. *United Communist Party of Turkey v Turkey*, at para 32.
56. *United Communist Party of Turkey v Turkey*, at para 57.
57. *Socialist Party of Turkey v Turkey*, Application 21237/93. Judgment of 25 May 1998.
58. *Socialist Party of Turkey v Turkey*, Application 21237/93. Judgment of 25 May 1998, at para 47.
59. *Freedom & Democracy Party (ÖZDEP) v Turkey*, Application 23885/94. Judgment of 8 December 1999.
60. *Refah Partisi (Welfare Party) v Turkey* (Applications 41340/98, 41342/98, 41343/98 and 41344/98). Grand Chamber Judgment of 13 February 2013.
61. *Refah Partisi (Welfare Party) v Turkey*, at para 47.
62. See, for example, *Refah Partisi (Welfare Party) v Turkey*, at para 102.
63. See, for example, *Herri Batasuna v Spain*, Applications 25803/04, 25817/04. Judgment of 30 June 2006; *Eusko Abertzale Ekintza–Acción Nacionalista Vasca (EAE–ANV) v Spain*, Application 40959/09. Judgment of 15 January 2013 and others.
64. European Commission for Democracy through Law (Venice Commission), *Guidelines on Prohibition of Political Parties and Analogous Measures* (1999). Adopted by the Venice Commission at its 41st Plenary session, 10–11 December 1999, Section 1.
65. *Partidul Communistilor (Nepeceristi) & Ungureanu v Romania*, Application 46626/99. Judgment of 3 February 2005.
66. *Linkov v Czech Republic*, Application 10504/03. Judgment of 7 December 2006.
67. *Artymov v Russian Federation*, Application 17582/05. Judgment of 7 December 2006.
68. *Christian Democratic People's Party v Moldova*, Application 28793/02. Judgment of 14 February 2006.
69. European Commission for Democracy through Law (Venice Commission), *Guidelines on Prohibition of Political Parties and Analogous Measures* (1999). Adopted by the Venice Commission at its 41st Plenary session, 10–11 December 1999, Section 1.
70. European Commission for Democracy through Law (Venice Commission), *Guidelines on Prohibition of Political Parties and Analogous Measures* (1999). Adopted by the Venice Commission at its 41st Plenary session, 10–11 December 1999.
71. European Commission for Democracy through Law (Venice Commission), *Guidelines on Prohibition of Political Parties and Analogous Measures* (1999). Adopted by the Venice Commission at its 41st Plenary session, 10–11 December 1999.
72. European Commission for Democracy through Law (Venice Commission), *Guidelines on Prohibition of Political Parties and Analogous Measures* (1999). Adopted by the Venice Commission at its 41st Plenary session, 10–11 December 1999.
73. Twenty-five states have ratified the American Convention on Human Rights: Argentina, Barbados, Bolivia, Brazil, Chile, Colombia, Costa Rica, the Dominican Republic, Ecuador, El Salvador, Grenada, Guatemala, Haiti, Honduras, Jamaica, Mexico, Nicaragua, Panama, Paraguay, Peru, Suriname, Trinidad and Tobago, Uruguay, and Venezuela.
74. SJ Schnably, "Constitutional and Democratic Government in the Inter-American System" in GH Fox and BR Roth (eds), *Democratic Governance and International Law* (Cambridge UP, Cambridge, 2000), 155–98.
75. Santiago Commitment to Democracy and the Renewal of the Inter-American System. Adopted by the General Assembly of OAS on 4 June 1991.
76. Representative Democracy. Resolution No 1080. Adopted by the General Assembly of OAS on 5 June 1991.
77. D Shelton, "The Jurisprudence of the Inter-American Court of Human Rights" (1994) 10(1) American U Int Law Rev 333–72, at 336.
78. Inter-American Commission of Human Rights, *Report on Terrorism and Human Rights*. (OEA/Ser. L/V/II.116. Doc. 5 rev. 1 corr, 2002), at para 359.
79. Inter-American Commission of Human Rights, *Report on Terrorism and Human Rights*. (OEA/Ser. L/V/II.116. Doc. 5 rev. 1 corr, 2002).

80. One of the examples would be the Inter-American Commission on Human Rights, *The Road to Substantive Democracy: Women's Political Participation in the Americas*. Special Report. (OEA/Ser.L/V/II. Doc.79, 2011).
81. *Baena Ricardo v Panama*. Judgment of 2 February 2002 at para 56; *Cantoral Huamani & Garcia Santa Cruz v Peru*. Judgment of 28 January 2008, at para 144; *Kawas Fernandez v Honduras*, Judgment of 3 April 2008 at para 143; *Escher v Brazil*, Judgment of 1 July 2009, at para 170.
82. *Escher v Brazil*, para 171.
83. *Escher v Brazil*.
84. *Yatama v Nicaragua*, Judgment of 23 June 2005.
85. A detailed commentary of this case and its implications is given in MS Campbell, "The Right of Indigenous Peoples to Political Participation and the Case of Yatama v. Nicaragua" (2007) 24(2) Arizona J of Int and Comp Law 499–540.
86. *Castaneda Gutman v Mexico*, Decision of 8 August 2006.
87. *Castaneda Gutman v Mexico*, Decision of 8 August 2006, at para 202.
88. R O'Connel, "Realising Political Equality: the European Court of Human Rights and Positive Obligations in a Democracy" () 61(3) NI Legal Quarterly 203–8, at 278.

Index

For Product Safety Concerns and Information please contact our EU representative GPSR@taylorandfrancis.com Taylor & Francis Verlag GmbH, Kaufingerstraße 24, 80331 München, Germany

Batch number: 10726294

Printed by Printforce, the Netherlands